st. NN → YY.

Spirited Cooking

With Liqueurs, Spirits and Wine

Sonia Allison

DAVID & CHARLES
Newton Abbot   London   North Pomfret (Vt)

Drawings by Robin Wiggins

British Library Cataloguing in Publication Data
Allison, Sonia
Spirited cooking
1. Cookery (Wine)
2. Cookery (Liquors)
I. Title
641.6′2   TX726
ISBN 0-7153-8015-X
Library of Congress Catalog Card Number 81-68254

Typeset by ABM Typographics Limited, Hull
Printed in Great Britain
by Butler & Tanner Limited, Frome & London
for David & Charles (Publishers) Limited
Brunel House   Newton Abbot   Devon
Published in the United States of America
by David & Charles Inc
North Pomfret   Vermont 05053   USA

Contents

Introduction

The idea of adding alcohol to food for special occasions is, as we all know, a good and long-established one. The idea of adding less conventional alcoholic drinks to fairly basic dishes is, I suspect, newer. It came to me when I viewed with increasing dismay my over-full cupboards bulging with bottles that had accrued over many years—the result of exploring bits of the world and bringing home tasters from everywhere, in the hope that friends and family would take the unusual opportunity of sampling a unique collection. Alas my hopes were dashed, guests sticking firmly to their gin-and-tonics, whisky-and-sodas, sherry or the occasional Campari; so I decided on a course of action. Instead of using up my lovely bottles on rare occasions for standards such as crêpes suzette and flaming the Christmas pudding, why not incorporate a dash of this and that in everyday cooking, and lift it from the mundane to Lucullian heights fit for connoisseurs of every age?

So I did just that and it worked like a charm, and for months and months we feasted on dishes laced with every conceivable tipple from Norwegian aquavit, cider and Galliano to Pernod, tawny port and white rum. My 'spirited cooking' developed style and panache and, apart from the actual cost of those gradually accumulated drinks, I was spending the same on ingredients as before. More importantly, the concoctions are fun to make, special to eat and, since the amounts of drink used are small, within the bounds of reality price-wise. Although I cannot claim that all the recipes are unique, I can vouch for their success—which I hope from time to time you will share with me, joining the ranks of culinary entrepreneurs. Thank you for listening and good luck!

Sonia Allison
Hertfordshire, 1981

Acknowledgements

The author would like to thank the many companies who supplied the following drinks: Amaretto di Saronno; Anisette, *Siebrand*; Aquavit, *Norwegian Linie, Danish Aalborg*; Apricot Brandy, *Siebrand, De Kuyper, Cusenier, Bols*; Bananes, Crème de, *Bols, Siebrand*; Cacao, Crème de, *Siebrand*; Cherry Heering; Cherry Marnier; Cherry Brandy, *De Kuyper, Cusenier, Grants, Siebrand*; Cocoribe; Coffee Whisky Liqueur, *Siebrand*; Cognac, *Bisquit, Prince Hubert de Polignac VSOP*; Cream Liqueur, *Siebrand*; Curaçao, *Cusenier*; Fraise, *Marie Brizard*; French Coffee Chocolate Liqueur, *Royal*; Galliano; Gin, *Beefeater*; Glayva; Grand Marnier; Kirsch; Kahlua; Mandarin, *Siebrand*; Menthe, Crème de, *Bols, Siebrand, Cusenier, (Freezomint)*; Pimm's No 1 Cup; Pimm's Cup (Vodka); Rum, *Lemon Hart Golden Jamaica, Lamb's Navy*; Sambuca Romana; Sherries, *Domecq*; Tequila, *Sauza, Siebrand Blanco*; Vodka, *Wyborowa, Stolichnaya, Smirnoff*.

Starters

Chilled Avocado Bean Soup

(*serves 6*)

A sumptuous soup to cool you down on a hot day.

2 large avocados
2 tbsp fresh lemon juice (3 tbsp)
1 slightly rounded tsp salt
1 garlic clove, peeled and crushed
½pt (275ml) cold chicken stock (1¼ cups)
½pt (275ml) cold water (1¼ cups)
1 tbsp gin (1½ tbsp)
6 level tbsp cooked green beans (9 tbsp cooked snap beans)
white pepper to taste

1 Peel avocados as you would peel a pear, starting from pointed end. Dice flesh directly into blender goblet.
2 Add lemon juice, salt, garlic and stock. Blend until smooth and purée-like. Pour into bowl.
3 Whisk in water. Cover. Refrigerate several hours until thoroughly chilled.
4 Before serving, stir in gin, beans and seasoning to taste.

Avocado and Vegetable 'Broth'

(*serves 6 to 8*)

6oz (175g) onions, peeled and chopped (¾ to 1 cup)
1 tbsp salad oil (1½ tbsp)
2 level tbsp flour (3 level tbsp all-purpose)
1pt (575ml) beef or chicken stock (2½ cups)
½ pt (275ml) tomato juice (1¼ cups)
2 level tsp salt (3 level tsp)
1 tsp Worcestershire sauce
6oz (175g) cooked green peas (about 1 cup)
8oz (225g) cooked white fish, flaked (about 1 cup)
1 large avocado
1 tbsp tequila (1½ tbsp)

1 Fry onions gently in oil until golden. Stir in flour to form roux. Gradually blend in stock and tomato juice. Bring to boil, stirring continuously.
2 Add salt, Worcestershire sauce and peas. Simmer 5 minutes. Stir in fish with peeled and diced avocado and tequila. Adjust seasoning to taste. Serve straight away.

Chilled Avocado Curry Soup

(serves 6)

Make soup exactly as in the Chilled Avocado Bean Soup using the first 6 ingredients plus 2 level tsp (3 level tsp) mild curry powder. Before serving, stir in 1 tsp Sambuca Romana, a few deep-fried onion rings and pepper to taste.

Cucumber Soup

(serves 6 to 8)

An enchantingly pretty, delicately-flavoured soup for summer entertaining.

2lb (900g) cucumber, peeled
1oz (25g) butter ($\frac{1}{8}$ cup)
1pt (575ml) chicken stock (2$\frac{1}{2}$ cups)
1 rounded tbsp cornflour (1$\frac{1}{2}$ rounded tbsp cornstarch)
$\frac{1}{2}$pt (275ml) cold milk (1$\frac{1}{4}$ cups)
1$\frac{1}{2}$ level tsp salt (about 2 level tsp)
white pepper to taste
2 tsp Sambuca Romana (3 tsp)

1 Finely grate cucumber then squeeze dry in clean tea towel to remove surplus water.
2 Heat butter in roomy saucepan. Add cucumber. Fry over minimal heat for 10 minutes. Keep pan covered throughout and stir occasionally.
3 Add stock. Bring slowly to boil. Reduce heat. Simmer 15 minutes. Blend to smooth purée, in 2 or 3 batches, in blender goblet. Return to pan.
4 Mix cornflour (cornstarch) smoothly with a little of the cold milk. Add remainder. Stir into cucumber soup.
5 Cook, stirring all the time, until soup comes to boil and thickens. Season. Simmer, uncovered, 5 minutes. Add Sambuca Romana. Serve very hot.

Chilled Tartan Soup

(serves 6)

An idea I had when my greengrocer offered me a box of 'borderline' tomatoes just after a kind heart in the drinks business had sent me a bottle of one of Scotland's finest liqueurs—Glayva. You will need a blender for this one.

1lb (450g) blanched tomatoes, skinned and quartered (about 6 medium)
1 carton (5fl oz or 142ml) soured cream ($\frac{5}{8}$ cup cultured soured cream)
1 medium-sized garlic clove, peeled and sliced
$1\frac{1}{2}$ level tsp salt (2 level tsp)
2 tbsp Glayva (3 tbsp)
$\frac{1}{2}$pt (275ml) water ($1\frac{1}{4}$ cups)
large pinch powdered mace or ground nutmeg
mustard and cress, chopped

1 Place tomatoes, in two batches, into blender goblet. Blend first batch on its own and tip into bowl. Blend second batch with soured cream, garlic and salt. Add to bowl.
2 Stir in Glayva, water and mace or nutmeg. Stir well to mix. Cover. Refrigerate a minimum of 4 hours.
3 Before serving, stir round and ladle into bowls. Sprinkle each with mustard and cress.

Chinese Omelet Shred Soup

(serves 6 to 8)

A light soup which makes a plausible beginning to a Chinese-style meal.

2 large eggs
$\frac{1}{2}$ level tsp salt ($\frac{3}{4}$ level tsp)
2pt (1·25 litres) chicken stock made with cubes and water (5 cups chicken bouillon)
1 tsp soy sauce ($1\frac{1}{2}$ tsp)
4oz (100 to 125g) cooked peas (1 cup)
2 tbsp medium sherry
salt to taste

1 Beat eggs with salt and make a thin omelet in usual way. Roll up. Cut into thin strips.
2 Pour stock (bouillon) into saucepan. Add rest of ingredients. Bring gently to boil. Simmer 2 to 3 minutes. Stir in omelet strips.
3 Heat a further 2 minutes. Ladle into warm bowls.

Canton Duckling Soup

(serves 6 to 8)

Worthwhile making during the Christmas season when you might have some spare duckling giblets.

2 sets duckling giblets, minus livers (2 sets duckling variety meats)
1 large onion, peeled and chopped
2pt (1·25 litres) water (5 cups)
1 tbsp soy sauce (1½ tbsp)
2 tbsp sweet sherry (3 tbsp)
1 can (8oz or 227g) water chestnuts, rinsed and halved
1 can (8oz or 227g) bamboo shoots, rinsed and coarsely chopped
1 level tsp salt

1 Place giblets or variety meats into saucepan. Add onion, water, soy sauce and sherry. Bring to boil.
2 Lower heat. Cover closely. Simmer 2 hours or until giblets are very soft. If necessary, top up with the occasional half teacup of boiling water.
3 Remove giblets or variety meats from soup. Finely cut up all the meat, first removing it from bones if necessary.
4 Return to soup with rest of ingredients. Heat through. Ladle into soup bowls. Serve piping hot.

Lettuce Soup

(serves 6)

Mildly flavoured with curry powder and medium-sweet sherry, this is a subtle, summer soup for any occasion. Try it hot with cheese straws, or chill in the refrigerator and serve each portion sprinkled with finely chopped chives.

3 medium-sized round lettuces
2oz (50g) butter ($\frac{1}{4}$ cup)
1 level tbsp cornflour ($1\frac{1}{2}$ level tbsp cornstarch)
1pt (575ml) chicken stock ($2\frac{1}{2}$ cups)
$\frac{1}{2}$ level tsp salt ($\frac{3}{4}$ level tsp)
2 tbsp medium-sweet sherry (3 tbsp)
1 level tsp curry powder ($1\frac{1}{2}$ level tsp)

1 Trim lettuces, discarding bruised outside leaves if necessary. Quarter each, then wash under gently running water. Shake dry. Cut lettuces into strips.
2 Heat butter. Add lettuce. Fry over low heat for 7 minutes, turning frequently. Sprinkle with cornflour and mix well.
3 Gradually blend in stock. Cook, stirring, until soup comes to boil and thickens. Lower heat. Cover. Simmer 30 minutes. Blend to smooth purée, in 2 or 3 batches, in blender goblet.
4 Return to pan. Season with salt. Bring slowly to boil again, stirring. Add sherry and curry powder. Stir. Serve hot or cold.

Pumpkin Soup with Chicken

(serves 6 to 8)

A golden, glowing soup with a lovely flavour. Try it on cold winter days and, if you want to stay vegetarian, omit the chicken.

1 can (14oz or 398ml) pumpkin purée or the equivalent made from freshly cooked pumpkin (about 2 cups)
$\frac{1}{2}$pt (275ml) milk ($1\frac{1}{4}$ cups)
1pt (575ml) chicken stock or vegetable water left over from cooking onions, carrots etc ($2\frac{1}{2}$ cups)

2 to 3 level tsp onion salt (3 to 4½ level tsp)
3 tbsp dry vermouth (4½ tbsp)
large pinch ground nutmeg
8oz (225g) cold, cooked chicken meat, cubed
chopped parsley

1 Spoon pumpkin purée into saucepan. Add milk, stock or vegetable water and onion salt.
2 Bring to boil, stirring. Lower heat. Cover. Simmer 5 minutes. Pour in vermouth. Season with nutmeg.
3 Continue to simmer 5 minutes without chicken; 15 minutes with chicken. Ladle into warm cups or bowls and sprinkle each with chopped parsley.

Chunky Spiced Tomato Soup

(serves 8)

Somewhat unusual, this is marvellous to make during the late summer months when the garden presents you with a glut of tomatoes. Filling and nutritious, make the soup a main course with crusty brown bread or rolls, and wedges of Caerphilly or red Leicester cheese.

1 tbsp salad oil (1½ tbsp)
6oz (175g) onions, peeled and chopped (about ¾ cup)
2oz (50g) bacon, chopped (2 bacon strips)
2lb (900g) blanched tomatoes, skinned and chopped (about 12 medium)
1 level tsp mixed herbs (1½ level tsp fines herbes)
3 level tsp salt (4½ level tsp)
1pt (575ml) hot water (2½ cups)
4 tbsp Dubonnet (6 tbsp)
3 large slices brown bread, made into crumbs
¼ level tsp cinnamon (same)
¼ level tsp ground coriander (same)
1 level tsp French mustard (1½ level tsp)

1 Heat oil in large pan. Add onions and bacon. Fry slowly about 7 to 10 minutes or until lightly browned.
2 Add all remaining ingredients. Stir well to mix. Bring to boil, stirring. Lower heat. Cover. Simmer 30 minutes. Stir round and serve.

British Mulligatawny Soup

(*serves 6*)

At the height of its popularity during the days of the Raj, this is a soup well worth reviving for its mild temperament and sweet-sour flavour. At least it's a change from Brown Windsor!

2oz (50g) butter or margarine, melted ($\frac{1}{4}$ cup)
2 medium-sized carrots, peeled and grated
1 large onion, peeled and grated
3 medium-sized celery stalks, well cleaned and thinly sliced
2oz (50g) flour ($\frac{1}{2}$ cup all-purpose)
3 level tsp Madras curry powder ($4\frac{1}{2}$ tsp)
$1\frac{1}{2}$pt (875ml) beef stock ($3\frac{3}{4}$ cups)
2 medium-sized cooking apples, peeled and grated
1 rounded tbsp seedless raisins ($1\frac{1}{2}$ rounded tbsp)
1 tbsp fresh lemon juice ($1\frac{1}{2}$ tbsp)
1 rounded tsp sugar ($1\frac{1}{2}$ rounded tsp)
1 rounded tsp salt ($1\frac{1}{2}$ rounded tsp)
3 tbsp dry sherry ($4\frac{1}{2}$ tbsp)
2oz (50g) cooked chicken, chopped (about $\frac{1}{2}$ cup)
4 rounded tbsp long grain rice, cooked (6 tbsp)
4 tbsp natural yogurt (6 tbsp)

1 Heat butter or margarine in large pan. Add carrots, onion and celery. Fry gently until light gold.
2 Stir in flour and curry powder to form roux. Cook 2 minutes. Gradually blend in stock. Bring to boil, stirring continuously. Add apples, raisins, lemon juice, sugar and salt.
3 Lower heat. Cover. Simmer 1 hour. Strain into clean pan. Add sherry. Reheat till very hot. Distribute chicken and rice between 6 soup bowls. Fill with soup. Top each with a spoon of yogurt.

Seafood Soup

(*serves 8*)

In the haute cuisine class, here is a memorable soup of distinction made from a simple fish stock (recipe below), seafood, dry white wine and brandy.

2oz (50g) butter ($\frac{1}{4}$ cup)

2oz (50g) flour ($\frac{1}{2}$ cup all-purpose)

1$\frac{1}{2}$pt (875ml) fish stock (3$\frac{3}{4}$ cups)

$\frac{1}{4}$pt (150ml) dry white wine ($\frac{5}{8}$ cup)

2 level tbsp tomato purée (3 level tbsp tomato paste)

1 carton (5fl oz or 142ml) soured cream ($\frac{5}{8}$ cup cultured soured cream)

1 level tsp salt (1$\frac{1}{2}$ level tsp)

4oz (125ml) peeled shrimps or prawns (about $\frac{3}{4}$ cup)

4oz (125ml) cooked flaked haddock or salmon (about $\frac{3}{4}$ cup)

4oz (125ml) canned tuna, drained and flaked (about $\frac{3}{4}$ cup)

3 tsp brandy (4$\frac{1}{2}$ tsp)

white pepper to taste

1 Melt butter in pan. Stir in flour to form roux. Cook 2 minutes without browning.
2 Gradually blend in fish stock. Bring to boil, stirring continually. Add wine, purée and soured cream. Whisk until smooth and soup bubbles gently.
3 Stir in all remaining ingredients. Heat through until very hot. Ladle into soup bowls. Accompany with cheese straws.

Fish Stock

Simmer 3pt (1$\frac{3}{4}$ litre) water (7$\frac{1}{2}$ cups) for 1 hour with 1 bouquet garni bag, 1 peeled and chopped onion, 1 peeled and sliced carrot, 1 large and coarsely chopped celery stalk, 8oz (225g) fish trimmings, a handful of parsley and 3 level tsp salt (4$\frac{1}{2}$ level tsp). Keep pan covered throughout. Strain before use.

Cauliflower Cream Soup with Watercress

(serves 6)

Light and creamy, this is an excellent soup to serve either hot or cold.

1 medium-sized cauliflower, all greenery discarded
½pt (150ml) milk (1¼ cups)
½pt (150ml) water (1¼ cups)
1 medium-sized onion, peeled and quartered
2 level tsp salt (3 level tsp)
1 tbsp white port or very dry sherry (1½ tbsp)
1oz (25g) butter (⅛ cup)
¼pt (150ml) single cream (⅝ cup coffee cream)
1oz (25g) watercress leaves, chopped (about ¼ cup, loosely packed)

1 Break cauliflower head into florets. Put into large pan with milk, water, onion and salt.
2 Bring to boil. Lower heat. Cover. Cook gently until vegetables are very soft.
3 Blend with liquid to smooth purée in blender goblet. Return to pan. Stir in port or sherry, butter and cream.
4 Bring just up to boil. Remove from heat. Stir round. Ladle into soup bowls. Sprinkle with watercress.

Note If serving cold, chill soup *before* sprinkling with watercress.

Christmas Soup

(serves 6 to 8)

Mellowed with port and cognac and laced with strips of cooked turkey, here is a perfect, short-cut soup for the festive season.

1 can (15½oz or 440g) unsweetened chestnut purée (2 cups)
½pt (275ml) chicken stock

4 tbsp ruby port (6 tbsp)
8oz (225g) cooked turkey, cut into strips (about 1½ cups)
1 level tsp salt (1½ level tsp)
1 tbsp cognac (1½ tbsp)

1 Spoon chestnut purée into saucepan. Stand over low heat. Gradually whisk in chicken stock. Bring slowly to boil.
2 Add port and turkey. Cover. Simmer 15 minutes. Season to taste. Pour cognac into small pan. Heat to lukewarm. Ignite. Stir into soup.
3 Adjust seasoning to taste then ladle into warm soup bowls. Serve piping hot.

Stilton Dip with Crudités

(serves about 8)

If you take the king of all cheeses, mix it with port and thick cream,
and serve it with raw vegetables to dip, you have a truly royal starter
for everybody's pleasure.

12oz (350g) Stilton cheese
¼pt (150ml) double cream (⅝ cup heavy cream)
1 small onion, peeled and very finely grated
4 tbsp ruby port (6 tbsp)
about 1 heaped tbsp chopped salted peanuts for garnish (about 1½ heaped tbsp)

1 Mash Stilton cheese finely then beat in cream and onion. When smooth and well blended, stir in port.
2 Transfer mixture to small serving bowl and sprinkle with nuts. Stand in the centre of a large platter surrounded with crudités comprising the following (for dipping) :-

radishes
sticks of unpeeled cucumber
sticks of peeled carrot
cauliflower florets
2in (5cm) lengths of celery
squares of red and green pepper

15

Smoked Mackerel Pâté with Gin

(serves 6 to 8)

A simple starter which is full of flavour and richness, and
especially well suited to strips of hot toast.

8oz (225g) smoked mackerel fillets, skinned
2 tbsp fresh lemon juice (3 tbsp)
1 medium-sized garlic clove, peeled and sliced
2 tsp gin (3 tsp)
1 tsp Worcestershire sauce (1½ tsp)
2oz (50g) butter, softened (¼ cup)

1 Flake up fish with two forks, discarding any bones. Place in blender goblet or food
processor.
2 Add all remaining ingredients. Run machine until ingredients form a purée, stopping
machine and scraping down sides once or twice.
3 Transfer to a small serving dish, smoothing top with knife. Cover with cling film.
Refrigerate until firm. Spoon out of dish to serve.

Prawns in the Newburg Style

(serves 4)

For luxury lovers!

1oz (25g) butter (⅛ cup)
12oz (350g) Norwegian peeled prawns
3 tbsp marsala (4½ tbsp)
1 tbsp brandy (1½ tbsp)
1 carton (5fl oz or 142ml) soured cream (⅝ cup cultured soured cream)
salt and white pepper to taste

1 Heat butter until foaming in frying pan. Add prawns. Fry over medium heat for 5
minutes.
2 Stir in all remaining ingredients. Continue to heat until mixture *just* comes to boil and
begins to bubble.
3 Mound equal amounts over freshly cooked rice and serve straight away.

Prawns Provençale

(serves 4)

A vivacious appetiser, generally served with fluffy rice. It takes minutes to make.

1 can (14oz or 396g) tomatoes (2 cups)
1 large garlic clove, peeled and crushed
2 rounded tbsp chopped parsley (3 rounded tbsp)
$\frac{1}{2}$ level tsp salt ($\frac{3}{4}$ level tsp)
12oz (350g) Norwegian peeled prawns
1 tbsp tequila ($1\frac{1}{2}$ tbsp)
1 level tsp sugar ($1\frac{1}{2}$ level tsp)

1 Place tomatoes in a saucepan and coarsely crush. Add garlic, parsley and salt.
2 Bring to boil, stirring. Lower heat. Cover. Simmer 15 minutes. Add prawns, tequila and sugar.
3 Stir well to mix. Heat through until bubbling. Serve straight away.

Smoked Salmon Pâté à la Russe

(serves 8 generously)

For this you can get away with salmon pieces (always cheaper than sliced) but it would be sheer extravagance to use best Scottish. If pieces are unavailable, use Canadian salmon. A food processor or blender is a must for this recipe.

8oz (225g) salmon pieces
1 tbsp vodka ($1\frac{1}{2}$ tbsp)
3 tsp lemon juice ($4\frac{1}{2}$ tsp)
4oz (125g) unsalted butter, softened ($\frac{1}{2}$ cup)
white pepper to taste
chopped fresh or dried dill, or chopped parsley

1 Place salmon pieces (skin and all bones removed) into food processor or blender.
2 Add vodka, lemon juice and butter. Run machine until mixture becomes smooth and pâté-like. Spoon out of bowl or goblet into basin.
3 Season with pepper. Spoon into a small soufflé dish. Cover. Refrigerate until firm. Sprinkle with dill or parsley. Spoon out of dish. Serve with hot toast.

Smoked Salmon Mousse

(serves 8)

More economical than serving smoked salmon by itself, Smoked Salmon Mousse is a novelty hors d'oeuvre, easily put together with the aid of a blender.

3 level tsp powdered gelatine (4½ level tsp unflavoured gelatin)
¼pt (150ml) cold water (⅝ cup)
8oz (225g) smoked salmon pieces
1 carton (5fl oz or 142ml) soured cream (⅝ cup cultured soured cream)
2 tsp Pernod (3 tsp)
1 tbsp lemon juice (1½ tbsp)
salt and pepper to taste
2 egg whites
chopped parsley

1 Tip gelatine into saucepan. Add water. Leave to soften 10 minutes. Stand over minimal heat until gelatine dissolves and liquid is clear. Cool to lukewarm.
2 Pour into blender. Add cut-up salmon pieces, making sure bones and any pieces of skin have been discarded.
3 Blend smoothly to purée. Spoon into basin. Beat in soured cream, Pernod and lemon juice. Season. Cover. Refrigerate until just beginning to thicken and set.
4 Beat egg whites to a stiff snow. Fold into salmon mixture, flipping mixture over and over until smooth.
5 Transfer to an attractive glass dish. Cover. Refrigerate until firm and set. Garnish with a border of parsley before serving.
6 To eat, spoon portions out onto plates and accompany with Melba toast or crackers.

Glayva Grapefruits

(serves 6)

Nothing pretentious here, but a new approach to a tried and trusted favourite.

3 large grapefruits
6 tbsp Glayva (9 tbsp)
soft brown sugar
6 red or green maraschino-flavour cocktail cherries

1 Halve grapefruits horizontally. Loosen flesh round sides with curved grapefruit knife then cut into segments.
2 Pour equal amounts of Glayva over each, then sprinkle with sugar. Refrigerate until cold but not chilled. Top with cherries before serving.

Salmon-stuffed Mushrooms

(serves 4)

Splendid this, but make sure you find those enormous, saucer-sized mushrooms to use as a base. Smaller mushrooms don't fit somehow.

4 large, flat mushrooms, each about 4oz (125g) and 4in (10cm) in diameter
milk
1 can (7½oz or 213g) red salmon
2 large slices white bread, turned into crumbs
3 tbsp single cream (4½ tbsp coffee cream)
2 tsp Pernod, or anisette liqueur if you like a touch of sweetness (3 tsp)
1 level tsp mustard powder (1½ level tsp)
2oz (50g) butter, melted (¼ cup)
2oz (50g) grated Swiss cheese (½ cup)

1 Trim mushrooms. Remove stalks and chop fairly finely. Place mushrooms in large frying pan or skillet. Cover with about 2in (5cm) milk.
2 Poach, covered, about 5 to 7 minutes or until mushrooms are only just tender. Carefully lift out of pan and remove to buttered grill pan.
3 Finely mash salmon and juice from can. Stir in crumbs, cream, Pernod or anisette, mustard and melted butter. Mix in chopped stalks.
4 Work in a little of the mushroom milk if stuffing seems a little on the dry side. Pile equal amounts on top of mushrooms.
5 Spread evenly with a knife then heap cheese on top of each. Grill 10 minutes, about 4in (10cm) from source of heat. Serve straight away.

Seafood Galettes

(*serves 8*)

The type of thing you could expect to find in northern France, and in Brittany
particularly with its multitude of assorted fish. In Britain, alas, one has
to compromise and buy what is available, but the selection of fish below gives
a fair copy of the original.

4oz (125g) plain flour (1 cup all-purpose)

pinch of salt

2 large eggs

1oz (25g) butter, melted ($\frac{1}{8}$ cup)

$\frac{1}{2}$pt (275ml) cold milk ($2\frac{1}{4}$ cups)

white vegetable fat for frying, melted (shortening)

Filling

2oz (50g) butter or margarine ($\frac{1}{4}$ cup)

2oz (50g) flour ($\frac{1}{2}$ cup)

$\frac{1}{2}$pt (275ml) fish stock ($2\frac{1}{4}$ cups), recipe on page 13

$\frac{1}{2}$pt (275ml) milk ($2\frac{1}{4}$ cups)

12oz (350g) peeled prawns

8oz (225g) lightly cooked scallops, diced

4oz (125g) cooked fresh salmon, flaked

2 tbsp brandy (3 tbsp)

salt and pepper to taste

Topping

3oz (75g) Gruyère cheese ($\frac{3}{4}$ cup)

1 To make pancakes, sift flour and salt into bowl. Beat in eggs, butter and half the milk.
Beat vigorously until smooth, allowing a good 10 minutes. Stir in rest of milk.

2 Cover. Refrigerate batter for 2 hours as this makes for more tender pancakes. To cook,
brush a large and heavy-based frying pan with white cooking fat (shortening). Heat
until hot. Pour in sufficient batter to form a thin pancake over base of pan.

3 Fry until golden. Turn over. Fry second side until brown and speckled. Repeat, using
rest of batter to make a total of 8 pancakes. Stack one on top of the other and stand on a
plate over a pan of hot water to keep warm.

4 For sauce, melt butter or margarine in pan. Stir in flour to form roux. Cook 1 minute.
Gradually blend in stock and milk.

5 Cook, stirring, until sauce comes to boil and thickens. Simmer 5 minutes. Add all remaining ingredients. Mix in well. Heat through until very hot.
6 Spread half the mixture over pancakes and roll up. Arrange side by side in buttered heatproof dish.
7 Coat with rest of filling mixture then sprinkle with cheese. Reheat in oven set to 400°F (200°C), Gas 6 for 15 minutes. Brown top by flashing under hot grill. Allow 1 per person.

Creamed Seafood Toasts with Sherry

(serves 6)

The sort of starter that can be made fairly quickly and easily from store cupboard ingredients.

1oz (25g) butter ($\frac{1}{8}$ cup)
1oz (25g) flour ($\frac{1}{4}$ cup)
$\frac{1}{4}$pt (150ml) apple juice ($\frac{5}{8}$ cup)
$\frac{1}{4}$pt (150ml) water ($\frac{5}{8}$ cup)
4 tbsp sherry (6 tbsp)
1 can (7oz or 198g) tuna, drained and flaked ($\frac{3}{4}$ cup)
2 tbsp double cream (3 tbsp heavy cream)
1 egg yolk
salt and pepper to taste
6 slices freshly made toast, stamped into large rounds with biscuit cutter (cookie cutter)
watercress for garnishing

1 Melt butter in pan. Stir in flour to form roux. Gradually blend in apple juice and water. Cook, stirring, until sauce comes to boil and thickens.
2 Stir in sherry and tuna. Heat through till bubbling. Stir in cream beaten with egg yolk, which will slightly thicken mixture.
3 Season to taste. Spoon onto toast. Garnish with watercress sprigs.

Stuffed Peppers in Pimm's

(serves 6)

A new turn up for the book; meat-filled peppers in a sauce tingling with vodka-based Pimm's.

6 medium-sized red peppers
1lb (450g) raw minced beef (16oz ground beef)
2oz (50g) easy cook rice (3 rounded tbsp)
2 garlic cloves, peeled and crushed
$\frac{1}{2}$pt (275ml) water (1$\frac{1}{4}$ cups)
4 tbsp Pimm's Cup, vodka-based (6 tbsp)
1 level tsp salt (1$\frac{1}{2}$ level tsp)

To cook
1pt (575ml) beef stock (2$\frac{1}{2}$ cups)
2 extra tbsp Pimm's as above (3 tbsp)

1 Wash and dry peppers. Cut off tops and reserve for lids. Remove inside fibres and seeds and discard.
2 Mix beef with rice, garlic, water, Pimm's and salt. Pack into peppers. Top with lids. Stand upright in pan.
3 Add stock and extra Pimm's. Bring to boil. Reduce heat. Cover. Simmer gently 45 minutes. Serve hot, each pepper coated with pan juices.

Braised Leeks

(serves 4)

Hot or cold, Braised Leeks make an inexpensive but appetising starter which will especially appeal to slimmers.

8 small to medium-sized leeks
$\frac{1}{4}$pt (150ml) chicken or beef stock ($\frac{5}{8}$ cup)
light sprinkle of salt
2 tbsp anisette liqueur (3 tbsp)
1 level tsp dried marjoram (1$\frac{1}{2}$ level tsp)

22

1 Trim leeks, leaving on 3in (7·5cm) green part. Slit lengthwise almost to crown and wash thoroughly between leaves.
2 Shake to remove surplus water. Place in oblong heatproof dish. Add stock. Sprinkle with last 3 ingredients.
3 Bring to boil over medium heat. Cover. Simmer gently about 30 to 35 minutes or until tender. Serve hot or cold with pan juices.

Celeriac in Gin Sauce

(*serves 6*)

Served in individual dishes or scallop shells, this makes an attractive and light starter which can be prepared one or two days ahead of time and reheated before serving.

2lb (900g) celeriac
1 to 2 level tsp salt (1½ to 3 level tsp)
2 tsp lemon juice (3 tsp)
1oz (25g) butter (⅛ cup)
1oz (25g) flour (¼ cup)
¼pt (150ml) milk (⅝ cup)
1 tbsp gin (1½ tbsp)
salt and pepper to taste
3oz (75g) Cheddar cheese, grated (¾ cup)
2 medium-sized tomatoes, sliced

1 Peel celeriac thickly and cut into thin slices. Place in large pan with water to cover. Add salt and lemon juice. Bring to boil. Lower heat.
2 Cover with lid and simmer 30 to 40 minutes or until celeriac is very tender. Drain, reserving ¼pt (150ml) celeriac water (⅝ cup).
3 To make sauce, melt butter in pan. Stir in flour to form roux. Cook 2 minutes without browning. Gradually blend in celeriac water and milk.
4 Cook, stirring, until sauce comes to boil and thickens. Add gin, replace celeriac and season to taste with salt and pepper. Reheat until hot. Divide equally between 6 individual, buttered heatproof dishes or buttered scallop shells.
5 Sprinkle with two-thirds of the cheese, top with tomato slices then sprinkle with rest of cheese. Brown under a hot grill.

Cranberry Melons

(serves 4)

I picked up this idea after a visit to Boston, home of cranberries, baked beans and a curious vegetable dish called Succotash which belongs to the Indians.

2 ripe melons
1 jar (6½oz or 185g) cranberry sauce (just under 1 cup)
2 tbsp tawny port (3 tbsp)
1 can mandarins, drained
maraschino-flavour cocktail cherries

1 Halve melons and remove inside seeds. Mix cranberry sauce with port. Spoon into melon cavities. Refrigerate on plates for 1 hour.
2 Before serving, decorate with 'kebabs' made from mandarins and cherries, threaded onto cocktail sticks (picks).

Creamed Mushrooms in the Central European Style

(serves 6)

A classic and smart starter from Poland which is unashamedly rich.

2oz (50g) butter (¼ cup)
1 large garlic clove, peeled and crushed
1lb (450g) button mushrooms (about 5 cups)
1 carton (5fl oz or 142ml) soured cream (⅝ cup cultured soured cream)
1 tbsp vodka (1½ tbsp)
salt and pepper to taste
chopped parsley

1 Melt butter slowly in large frying pan or skillet. Add garlic. Fry gently about 5 minutes when butter should be very hot and just beginning to turn brown.
2 Add all the mushrooms. Fry briskly 3 to 4 minutes, turning all the time. Stir in cream and vodka. Heat through quickly.
3 Season. Spoon onto 6 warm plates. Sprinkle with parsley.

Marinaded Mushrooms

(*serves 6 to 8*)

With a distinct, musky aroma of woods and forests, raw mushrooms in a zesty marinade give a fresh start to any meal. Try this old favourite recipe of mine and see what you think.

1½lb (675g) trimmed button mushrooms
2 medium-sized garlic cloves, peeled
1 level tsp finely grated lemon peel (1½ level tsp)
6 tbsp salad oil (9 tbsp)
2 tbsp mild vinegar (3 tbsp)
1 tbsp Bénédictine, Drambuie or Yellow Izarra (1½ tbsp)
large pinch of mixed spice
1 level tsp dried marjoram (1½ level tsp)
salt and papper to taste
1 heaped tbsp chopped parsley (1½ heaped tbsp)

1 Slice mushrooms and put into large bowl. Crush garlic directly into another basin; add lemon peel, oil, vinegar, liqueur, spice and marjoram.
2 Season to taste with salt and pepper. Pour over mushrooms. Stir to mix. Leave to stand in the kitchen for 2 to 3 hours. Stir to mix again before serving.
3 Spoon onto plates. Sprinkle with parsley. Accompany with brown bread and butter.

Artichoke Hearts with Tequila Egg Dressing

(serves 4)

A vibrant-flavoured, rustic and more unusual starter for the height of summer.
Serve with wedges of crusty French bread or Greek style sesame rolls.

1 can (about 2oz or 50g) anchovy fillets in oil
$\frac{1}{4}$pt (150ml) olive oil ($\frac{5}{8}$ cup)
4 tbsp tarragon vinegar (6 tbsp)
2 level tsp Dijon mustard (3 level tsp)
2 tsp tequila (3 tsp)
2 hard boiled eggs, shelled and chopped (2 hard cooked eggs)
8 canned artichoke hearts, well drained
8 black olives

1 Place anchovies with their oil, the olive oil, vinegar, mustard and tequila into blender
goblet or food processor. Run either machine until dressing is smoothly blended.
2 Pour into jug. Stir in eggs. Arrange artichoke hearts on 4 individual plates.
3 Coat with dressing. Top attractively with olives. Serve straight away.

Milanese Risotto

(serves 8)

I had a peep behind the scenes in a famous restaurant about two hours drive away from Milan, and my eyes came out on stalks at the sight of local pale-beige truffles, slabs of Parmesan cheese, mounds of butter, endless bottles of wine and every imaginable variety of pasta. But my interest, at that moment, was in the risotto, and the lovely Mama in charge of the kitchen allowed me in to see how it was done. The result is this authentic recipe.

$\frac{1}{4}$ tsp saffron stamens (same)

2 tbsp boiling water (3 tbsp)

4oz (125g) butter ($\frac{1}{2}$ cup)

1 tbsp olive oil ($1\frac{1}{2}$ tbsp)

1 medium-sized onion, peeled and finely grated

1lb (450g) round grain Italian rice (easy cook if you can find it)

3pt (1·75 litres) chicken stock ($7\frac{1}{2}$ cups)

$\frac{1}{2}$pt (275ml) dry white Italian wine ($1\frac{1}{4}$ cups)

3 level tsp salt ($4\frac{1}{2}$ level tsp)

1 tbsp brandy ($1\frac{1}{2}$ tbsp)

6oz (175g) grated Parmesan cheese

1 Put saffron into small dish. Add water. Leave to soak 15 minutes.
2 Heat half the butter and all the oil in large pan. Add onion. Cover pan. Cook over minimal heat about 12 to 15 minutes or until soft but not coloured.
3 Uncover. Stir in rice, saffron mixture and half the stock. Bring to boil. Lower heat. Cover. Cook 20 minutes. Stirring gently all the time, add small amounts of remaining stock over a period of about 15 minutes. Add wine and salt. Continue to cook and stir a further 10 minutes when rice should be tender but identifiable as grains. The liquid at this stage should be creamy looking and fairly thick.
4 Stir in brandy, rest of butter and three-quarters of the cheese which will thicken the Risotto even more. Adjust seasoning to taste. Spoon out onto warm plates and sprinkle rest of cheese on top of each. Serve straight away.

Rice Romana

(serves 4)

A zingy starter which is bright, colourful and appetising.

8oz (225g) long grain rice, freshly cooked (1¼ cups)
1 large, ripe avocado
2 heaped tbsp pickled red pepper, chopped (3 heaped tbsp)
6oz (175g) cooked gammon, diced (1 cup)

Dressing
2 tbsp red wine (3 tbsp)
1 tbsp red wine vinegar (1½ tbsp)
1 tsp Sambuca Romana (1½ tsp)
½ level tsp mustard powder (¾ level tsp)
1 tsp soy sauce (1½ tsp)
½ level tsp salt (¾ level tsp)

To Serve
4 lettuce leaves

1 Tip rice into bowl. Peel avocado as you would peel a pear, starting at the pointed end. Cut flesh into dice.
2 Add to rice with pickled pepper and diced gammon. Toss lightly.
3 For dressing, whisk ingredients well together. Pour over rice mixture. Toss again.
4 Line 4 individual plates with lettuce. Top with rice mixture. Serve.

Scandinavian Liver Paste

(serves about 8)

A beauty of a pâté—or paste as it is called—from the lands of the midnight sun. You'll find the uncooked mixture fairly slack, but it does thicken up when cooked and solidifies when cold.

1lb (450g) lamb or pork liver
1 medium-sized onion, peeled
4 level tbsp plain flour (6 level tbsp)

2oz (50g) butter or margarine, melted ($\frac{1}{4}$ cup)

1 large egg, beaten

6 tbsp double cream (9 tbsp heavy cream)

2 tbsp aquavit (3 tbsp)

$\frac{1}{4}$ level tsp ground allspice ($\frac{3}{4}$ level tsp)

1$\frac{1}{2}$ level tsp salt (2$\frac{1}{4}$ level tsp)

white pepper to taste

1 Wash liver and mince finely. Mince onion and add. Stir in flour, butter or margarine, egg, cream, aquavit, allspice, salt and pepper.

2 Beat until smooth. Pour into 2lb (1kg) loaf tin (4 cup capacity oblong loaf pan) lined with well greased foil. Cover with more greased foil.

3 Bake 2$\frac{1}{4}$ to 2$\frac{1}{2}$ hours in oven set to 325°F (160°C), Gas 3. To test if paste is set, uncover and push a cocktail stick (pick) into centre. If it comes out clean, remove tin (pan) from oven. If not, cook a further 15 to 30 minutes.

4 Cool in the tin. Turn out. Peel away paper. Refrigerate about 2 hours before slicing and serving with lettuce and tomato.

Blender Chicken Pâté

(serves about 8)

Smooth, creamy and rippled with cognac, this is a perfect pâté for those who like a classy starter to set the tone of a fine meal.

3oz (75g) butter ($\frac{3}{8}$ cup)

2 medium-sized garlic cloves, peeled and sliced

1 large onion, peeled and finely chopped

8oz (225g) chicken livers, well washed and drained (same)

large pinch mixed spice

2 level tsp salt (3 level tsp)

1 tbsp cognac (1$\frac{1}{2}$ tbsp)

1 Heat butter in large pan. Add garlic and onion. Fry very gently until pale gold.

2 Add livers gradually. Fry slowly about 30 minutes, or until cooked through. Allow a little longer if any of the livers still look pink.

3 Blend smoothly in two or three batches in blender goblet. Spoon out into bowl. Season with spice. Work in salt (using a little less if preferred) and the cognac.

4 Spread smoothly into small dish. Cover with cling film. Refrigerate until firm. Spoon out onto plates. Accompany with hot toast.

Flaming Wine-and-dine Kidneys

(serves 8)

Served with triangles of puff pastry (easily made from packeted varieties), this is a winner of a starter with a rotund flavour and colour to match.

1oz (25g) butter or margarine ($\frac{1}{8}$ cup)
2 tsp salad oil (3 tsp)
1 large onion, peeled and finely chopped
1lb (450g) lamb or pig kidney, cut into very small cubes
$\frac{1}{4}$pt (150ml) red wine ($\frac{5}{8}$ cup)
1 level tsp French or German mustard (1$\frac{1}{2}$ level tsp)
1 level tbsp tomato purée (1$\frac{1}{2}$ level tbsp tomato paste)
2 level tsp salt (3 level tsp)
2 level tbsp cornflour (3 level tbsp cornstarch)
6 tbsp cold water (9 tbsp)
2 tbsp aquavit (3 tbsp)
2 heaped tbsp finely chopped parsley (3 heaped tbsp)

1 Heat butter or margarine and oil in pan. Add onion. Fry until golden brown. Stir in kidney cubes. Fry fairly briskly until well sealed.
2 Pour in wine. Add mustard, purée and salt. Bring to boil, stirring. Lower heat. Cover. Simmer gently 40 minutes.
3 Mix cornflour to thin cream with some of the water. Add rest of water. Pour into kidneys. Bring to boil, stirring, until sauce thickens. Simmer 5 minutes.
4 Heat aquavit to lukewarm. Pour over kidneys. Ignite. Serve when flames have subsided. Sprinkle each portion with parsley.

Marsala Livers

(serves 6)

A rich galaxy of a starter which teams best with hot toast made from brown bread. Alternatively, serve the livers with Milanese Risotto (page 27).

1 tbsp olive oil (1$\frac{1}{2}$ tbsp)
1lb (450g) chicken livers (16oz), washed and paper-dried
2 medium-sized garlic cloves, peeled and sliced

1 level tbsp cornflour (1½ level tbsp cornstarch)
¼pt (150ml) cold water (⅝ cup)
1 level tbsp tomato purée (1½ level tbsp tomato paste)
2 tbsp marsala (3 tbsp)
1 level tsp salt (1½ level tsp)
1 rounded tsp French mustard (1½ rounded tsp)

1 Heat oil in pan which is broad-based rather than tall and narrow. Add livers and garlic. Fry fairly briskly until well browned.
2 Reduce heat. Fry gently, uncovered, a further 30 minutes. Turn frequently to prevent burning.
3 Mix cornflour (cornstarch) smoothly with a little cold water. Add rest of water. Add to livers with tomato purée (paste). Bring slowly to boil, stirring.
4 Lower heat. Cover pan. Simmer 15 minutes. Add marsala, salt and mustard. Mix in well. Heat through to boiling. Serve hot.

Avocado Patchwork Cocktails

(*serves 6*)

1 level tbsp gelatine (1½ level tbsp unflavoured powdered gelatin)
4 tbsp cold water (6 tbsp)
1pt (575ml) tomato juice (2½ cups)
1 tsp Worcestershire sauce
1½ level tsp salt (2 level tsp)
1 tbsp bacardi (1½ tbsp)
2 large ripe avocados
1 tbsp lemon juice (1½ tbsp)
watercress and lemon slices for garnish

1 Shower gelatine into cold water. Stir round to mix. Leave to stand 5 minutes. Transfer to small pan. Heat gently until completely melted, but do not allow to boil.
2 Combine with tomato juice, sauce, salt and bacardi. Pour into bowl. Cover. Refrigerate until just beginning to thicken and set.
3 Peel each avocado as you would peel a pear, starting from the pointed end. Dice flesh into fairly small pieces. Toss with lemon juice.
4 Stir gently into tomato mixture then spoon mixture evenly into 6 wine-type glasses or small dishes. Return to the refrigerator and leave until firm and set. Garnish with watercress and lemon slices before serving.

Cheese Soufflé in the Grand Style

(*serves 8*)

One of the tall brigade, this one, and as fluffy and light as a summer cloud.

2oz (50g) butter or margarine (¼ cup)
2oz (50g) flour (½ cup all-purpose)
1 level tsp mustard powder (1½ level tsp)
½pt (275ml) milk (1¼ cups)
6oz (175g) Cheddar cheese, very finely grated (1½ cups)
4 medium-sized eggs, separated (kitchen temperature)
3 tsp Pernod, raki or ouzo (4½ tsp)
½ level tsp salt (¾ level tsp)

1 Thickly butter a 2½pt (1·5 litre) straight-sided glass or pottery soufflé dish (6¼ cup). To prevent the mixture from collapsing as it rises and spilling down the sides, tie a 6in (15cm) strip of non-stick paper securely round outside, making sure it extends about 4in (10cm) above rim of dish.

2 Heat butter or margarine in pan. Stir in flour and mustard to form roux. Cook about 1 minute without browning. Gradually blend in milk. Cook, stirring, until mixture thickens sufficiently to leave sides of pan clean and form a ball in centre of pan.

3 Beat in cheese, egg yolks, alcohol and salt. Whisk egg whites to a stiff snow. Using a balloon whisk or large metal spoon, gently and lightly fold into cheese mixture. This process should be carried out slowly as speed often results in beating and loss of air.

4 Pour into soufflé dish. Bake 45 minutes in oven set to 375°F (190°C), Gas 5. Do not open oven door at all or soufflé will fall. Serve straight away.

(*Top left*) Avocado and Vegetable 'Broth', (*right*) Avocado Bean Soup, (*below*) Avocado Curry Soup, recipes on pages 6–7 (*South African Avocados*)

(*Below*) Braised Mackerel Farci, recipe on page 40 (*Colman's Mustard*)

Beef Tartare in Avocado Shells

(serves 8)

Sent to me from South Africa, this unusual marriage of avocados
with Beef Tartare makes for happy summer eating and proves a
highly original and appetising starter. The essentials for
success are top-quality steak and avocados that are just
ripe. By the way, Beef Tartare *is* always served and eaten
uncooked. I hope that answers all the queries I've had before!

2lb (900g) rump steak, fat trimmed (2lb beef round steak)
4oz (125g) onion, peeled and grated (1 large onion)
4 heaped tbsp chopped parsley (6 tbsp)
1½ level tsp salt (2 tsp)
4 ripe avocados
lemon juice
8 tsp dark rum (12 tsp)
8 egg yolks
lettuce leaves

Accompaniments
capers
freshly milled pepper
Tabasco and Worcestershire sauce
lemon wedges
gherkins

1 Finely mince steak. Mix with onion, parsley and salt.
2 Peel avocados. Halve. Remove and discard stones. Brush flesh inside and out with
 lemon juice to prevent browning. Pour rum into each hollow.
3 Fill avocados with meat mixture. Make a slight indentation in each and drop in an egg
 yolk. Stand on lettuce lined plates.
4 Serve with listed accompaniments for people to help themselves and add to meat and
 avocado mixture accordingly.

Beef Tartare in Avocado Shells (*South African Avocados*)

Cauliflower Prawn Cheese

(serves 6)

A new variation on an old theme which serves as a reasonably priced starter with an elegant look.

1 medium-sized cauliflower
1oz (25g) butter ($\frac{1}{8}$ cup)
1oz (25g) flour ($\frac{1}{4}$ cup)
$\frac{1}{4}$pt (150ml) milk ($\frac{5}{8}$ cup)
2 tbsp tawny port (3 tbsp)
$\frac{1}{2}$ level tsp salt ($\frac{3}{4}$ level tsp)
1 level tsp French mustard ($1\frac{1}{2}$ level tsp)
8oz (225g) peeled prawns ($1\frac{1}{2}$ cups)
1 level tbsp chopped parsley ($1\frac{1}{2}$ level tbsp)
3 heaped tbsp grated Edam or Gouda cheese ($4\frac{1}{2}$ heaped tbsp)

1 Cook cauliflower in boiling salted water until tender. Drain, reserving $\frac{1}{4}$pt (150ml) cauliflower water. Keep cauliflower warm.
2 To make sauce, melt butter in pan. Stir in flour to form roux. Cook 2 minutes without browning.
3 Gradually blend in cauliflower water and milk. Cook, stirring, until sauce comes to the boil and thickens. Add port, salt and mustard. Stir in prawns and parsley. Remove from heat.
4 Divide cauliflower into florets and place in 6 well buttered, heatproof dishes. Coat with sauce. Sprinkle with cheese. Brown under a hot grill. Serve straight away.

Party Spaghetti Bolognese

A rich, lively and typically Italian ragù sauce, for spooning atop spaghetti.
This version is flavoured with dark rum, although Marsala may be used if
preferred.

2lb (900g) lean minced beef (2lb ground beef)

1 can (1lb 12oz or 794g) tomatoes (3½ cups)

4oz (125g) gammon, chopped (about ¾ cup Canadian bacon)

2 large garlic cloves, peeled and crushed

4 rounded tbsp tomato purée (6 rounded tbsp tomato paste)

4 tbsp navy rum (6 tbsp)

1 level tsp salt (1½ level tsp)

1 rounded tsp dried oregano (1½ rounded tsp)

½pt (275ml) water (1¼ cups)

1lb (450g) spaghetti, freshly cooked

grated Parmesan cheese for serving

1 Place meat in large frying pan or skillet. Fry over brisk heat until well browned and
crumbly, breaking it up with a fork all the time.
2 Drain off excess fat and discard. Add tomatoes (crushing whole ones down with fork),
gammon, garlic, tomato purée, rum, salt, oregano and water. Stir well to mix.
3 Bring to boil, stirring. Lower heat. Cover. Simmer 1½ hours, stirring occasionally.
4 Heap spaghetti on to warm plates. Top with ragù sauce. Pass cheese separately.

Hot Crab Pies

(*serves 6*)

Although based on pastry, the little crab pies are very different from conservative vol-au-vents, and two per person make a tasty and sustaining starter if the courses to follow are light.

12oz (350g) shortcrust pastry (pie crust), already prepared

Filling

½oz (15g) butter (2 tsp)

½oz (15g) flour (3 level tsp all-purpose)

¼pt (150ml) single cream (⅝ cup coffee cream)

1 tbsp cognac (1½ tbsp)

1 can (7oz or 198g) crab, drained and flaked (about 1¼ cups)

1 can (1½oz or 42g) dressed crab (about ⅓ cup)

salt and pepper to taste

beaten egg for brushing

1 Roll out pastry thinly. Cut into 12 rounds with a 3in (9cm) cutter and 12 rounds with a 2½in (6cm) cutter. Use larger rounds to line 12 individual bun tins (patty pans).

2 For filling, melt butter in pan. Stir in flour to form roux. Gradually blend in cream. Cook, stirring, until sauce comes to boil and thickens. Remove from heat.

3 Stir in crab, dressed crab and cognac. Season. Cool. Spoon equal amounts into lined pastry tins (pans).

4 Moisten lids with water. Place on top of pies, pinching edges together to join. Brush with egg for golden glaze. Bake 20 to 25 minutes, or until golden, in oven set to 425°F (220°C), Gas 7. Remove from tins and serve straight away.

Main Dishes

Braised Mackerel Farci

(serves 4)

A gourmet mackerel dish, cooked with wine and the merest trace of Pernod to add a dash of novelty to a top favourite fish.

4 average-sized mackerel, cleaned and boned
2oz (50g) fresh white or brown breadcrumbs (½ cup)
2oz (50g) dried apricots, washed and cut into small pieces with scissors (⅓ cup)
1 level tsp mixed herbs (1½ level tsp fines herbes)
1 level tsp mustard powder (1½ level tsp)
salt and pepper to taste
beaten egg to bind stuffing
¼pt (150ml) dry white wine (⅝ cup)
2 tsp Pernod (3 tsp)
1 small onion, peeled and sliced
1 large tomato, sliced
1oz (25g) butter or margarine, melted

1 Wash mackerel, dry inside and out with paper towels. Leave on one side temporarily.
2 To make stuffing, mix crumbs with apricots, herbs, mustard and seasoning to taste. Using a fork, bind loosely with beaten egg.
3 Pack equal amounts of stuffing into each mackerel. Place in heatproof dish. Coat with wine and Pernod. Sprinkle with extra salt and pepper, then top with onion slices and tomato. Trickle with butter or margarine.
4 Cover dish with lid or greased foil. Bake for 35 to 40 minutes in oven set to 375°F (190°C), Gas 5. Remove from oven and uncover. Serve from the dish with jacket potatoes and seasonal vegetables or salad.

Cod and Bacon Casserole

(*serves 6*)

Easy to put together, this flavour-rich fish dish has about it a touch of the exotic and yet is composed of fairly standard ingredients available everywhere.

1oz (25g) butter or margarine ($\frac{1}{8}$ cup)

8oz (225g) lean bacon in one piece, cut into small·cubes

2 medium-sized onions, peeled and cut into quarters

3 level tsp prepared English mustard ($4\frac{1}{2}$ level tsp)

1 large can (about 1lb 12oz or 400g) peeled tomatoes (about 4 cups)

3 tbsp gin (3 tbsp)

pepper to taste and salt if necessary

$1\frac{1}{2}$lb ($\frac{3}{4}$kg) skinned cod fillet, cut into 2in (5cm) cubes

1 large green pepper, de-seeded and cut into rings

2 tbsp salad oil (3 tbsp)

1 large garlic clove, crushed

1oz (25g) soft white breadcrumbs ($\frac{1}{2}$ cup)

1 Heat butter or margarine in large flameproof pan or skillet. Add bacon and onion quarters. Fry gently in covered pan until pale gold and soft, about 15 minutes.
2 Stir in mustard, tomatoes and gin. Bring to boil, stirring. Season to taste, taking care with salt as the bacon itself will add its own share to the contents. Reduce heat.
3 Add fish to tomato mixture. Cover. Simmer slowly for 10 minutes or until fish is white and flakes easily with a fork.
4 Add all except 3 green pepper rings to pan or skillet. Cook 5 minutes. Meanwhile heat oil in pan. Add garlic and crumbs. Fry until golden. Stir into fish and tomato mixture, taking care not to break up fish.
5 Top with reserved pepper rings and serve with boiled potatoes tossed in butter, and a green salad.

Plaice and Pasta Casserole

(serves 4)

An all-in-one dish which goes admirably with either cooked vegetables or a mixed salad.

5oz (150g) small pasta such as shells (1¼ cups)
½pt (275ml) boiling water (1¼ cups)
¼pt (150ml) cider (⅝ cup apple cider)
1 level tsp salt (1½ level tsp)
2 tsp Galliano (3 tsp)
1 bouquet garni bag
4 large white-skinned plaice fillets (flounder)
1oz (25g) butter, melted (⅛ cup)
3oz (75g) Cheddar cheese, grated (¾ cup)
½ level tsp paprika (¾ level tsp)

1 Mix together pasta, water, cider, salt, Galliano and bouquet garni bag. Place in large, buttered heatproof dish, preferably shallow and oblong in shape.
2 Arrange fish fillets in a single layer on top of pasta, placing them head end to tail alternately so that they form a neat line.
3 Coat with butter. Sprinkle with cheese followed by paprika. Cook, uncovered 30 minutes in oven set to 425°F (220°C), Gas 7. Remove bouquet garni bag before serving.

Snow Princess Fish Pie

(serves 4 to 6)

Soft as snow and immensely tasty, this novel fish dish is highly recommended for adventurous entertaining.

¾pt (425ml) freshly made white coating sauce (1½ cups)
12oz (350g) cooked white fish, flaked (about 2½ cups)
1 can (7oz or 198g) tuna, drained and flaked
2 level tsp mild curry powder (3 level tsp)
1 tbsp boiling water (1½ tbsp)
3 level tsp ouzo, raki or Pernod (4½ tsp)
1½ level tsp salt (2 level tsp)

42

Snow Potatoes

2lb (1kg) peeled potatoes, freshly boiled

2 rounded tbsp low-fat dried milk powder (3 rounded tbsp)

$\frac{1}{4}$pt (150ml) boiling water ($\frac{5}{8}$ cup)

1 medium-sized egg, separated

1 level tbsp toasted coconut (1$\frac{1}{2}$ level tbsp)

1 Stand sauce over low heat. Reheat until bubbling. Stir in fish gently.

2 Mix curry powder to paste with boiling water. Add to fish mixture with rest of ingredients. Cover. Leave over minimal heat.

3 Finely mash potatoes. Beat in powdered milk and water. Add egg yolk. Beat until potatoes are snow-like and fluffy. Leave over low heat.

4 Whisk egg white to stiff snow. Fold into potato mixture. Transfer fish to warm serving dish. Swirl potatoes over top. Sprinkle with coconut. Serve straight away and accompany with green vegetables to taste.

Smoked Cod à la Crème

(*serves 6*)

Sophisticated, light and perfect as a luncheon or supper
dish, either on toast or accompanied by freshly cooked long
grain rice, forked with butter and seasoned gently with
tarragon. Notice how the gin brings out the full flavour
of the fish and hints at distinction.

2oz (50g) butter or margarine ($\frac{1}{4}$ cup)

2oz (50g) flour ($\frac{1}{2}$ cup all-purpose)

$\frac{3}{4}$pt (425ml) fish stock as overleaf (1$\frac{7}{8}$ cups)

1 carton (5oz or 142ml) soured cream ($\frac{5}{8}$ cup cultured soured cream)

2 tbsp gin (3 tbsp)

1lb (450g) smoked cod or haddock, cooked and flaked (16oz finnan haddie)

3 shakes cayenne pepper

salt to taste if necessary

1 Melt butter or margarine in heavy-based pan. Stir in flour to form roux. Cook 2 minutes over low heat but do not allow to brown.

2 Gradually blend in fish stock. Cook, stirring, until sauce comes to boil and thickens. Whisk in cream.

3 Stir in gin, fish and cayenne pepper. Reheat, stirring as little as possible, until very hot. Season with salt if necessary. Serve straight away.

Saffron Fish Stock

Simmer 1lb (450g) fish trimmings (16oz) in 3pt (1·75 litres) water (7½ cups) with 2 large peeled onions, 1 bouquet garni bag, 4 saffron strands, 1 bay leaf, 2 cloves and 4 level tsp salt (6 level tsp). Allow to cook about 1½ hours and keep pan covered all the time. Strain. Use as required. Store leftovers in the fridge up to 3 days or in the deep freeze up to 3 months.

Vermouth Baked Stuffed Haddock

(serves 4)

Fish topped with a crunchy nut stuffing, then baked with dry vermouth and butter until tender and flaky.

3oz (75g) brown breadcrumbs (¾ cup)
2oz (50g) salted peanuts, finely chopped (½ cup)
1 level tsp mixed herbs (1½ level tsp fines herbes)
1 level tsp onion salt (1¼ level tsp)
2 rounded tbsp chopped parsley (3 rounded tbsp)
1 medium-sized egg
2 tbsp milk (3 tbsp)
salt and pepper to taste
4 fillets of skinned haddock, each 6oz or 150g
2oz (50g) butter, melted (¼ cup)
¼pt (150ml) dry vermouth (⅝ cup)
peeled orange slices to garnish

1 Mix crumbs with peanuts, herbs, onion salt and parsley. Fork mix together with unbeaten egg and milk.
2 Stand fish in buttered heatproof dish. Spread evenly with breadcrumb mixture. Trickle melted butter over each. Pour vermouth into dish.
3 Bake, uncovered, 30 to 35 minutes in oven set to 425°F (220°C), Gas 7, basting twice. Transfer to 4 warm plates, garnish with orange slices and coat with pan juices. Accompany with creamed potatoes and cooked vegetables to taste.

Fish Kebabs

(serves 8)

Slightly oriental, these characterful kebabs look and taste
exotic, yet are made from easy-to-find and inexpensive ingredients.
Fatless, too, so low in cholesterol.

3 level tbsp clear honey (4½ tbsp)
3 tbsp tequila (4½ tbsp)
4 tbsp lemon juice (6 tbsp)
2 tbsp light variety soy sauce (3 tbsp)
¼ level tsp chilli powder
6 medium-sized herring, trout or whiting, gutted but left whole
3 medium-sized onions, peeled and sliced
8 courgettes, cut into 1in (2·5cm) slices (zucchini)
2 large lemons, washed dried and sliced

1 For marinade and, subsequently, glaze, combine honey, tequila, lemon juice, soy sauce
and chilli powder in small pan. Warm and stir until well blended.

2 Remove heads and tails from fish and discard. Cut fish into 1½in (3·75cm) chunks.
Thread onto 8 skewers alternately with onion slices, courgettes (zucchini) and lemons.

3 Arrange in shallow dish. Baste with honey mixture. Leave to marinate for 30 minutes,
turning over twice.

4 Stand in preheated grill pan. Brush with marinade. Grill 7 minutes. Turn over. Brush
with more marinade. Continue to grill a further 8 minutes or until all ingredients are
cooked through and golden. Brush frequently with leftover marinade throughout
grilling.

5 Serve straight away with a large mixed salad and either freshly cooked rice or crusty
pieces of new bread.

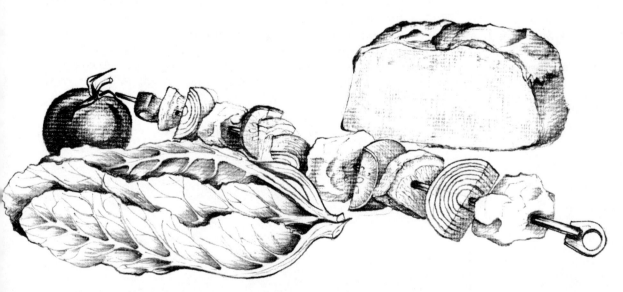

Chicken Crisp with Sherry Gravy

(*serves 4*)

Peanut butter and chopped peanuts add a lively note to roast
chicken portions and convert them from an ordinary dish into
something special.

4 large chicken portions
1oz (25g) butter, melted (1½ tbsp)
salt and pepper
5 level tbsp smooth peanut butter (7½ tbsp)
4 rounded tbsp salted peanuts, finely chopped (6 tbsp)
2 rounded tbsp chopped parsley (3 rounded tbsp)

Gravy
1 heaped tbsp flour (1½ tbsp all-purpose)
½pt (275ml) chicken stock (1¼ cups)
2 tbsp dry sherry (3 tbsp)
salt and pepper to taste

Garnish
lemon slices
watercress

1 Wash and dry chicken portions. Place in roasting tin (pan), skin sides uppermost. Brush
  with butter. Sprinkle with salt and pepper.
2 Cover tin (pan) with a 'lid' of foil. Cook 40 minutes in oven set to 350°F (180°C), Gas 4.
  Uncover. Spread with peanut butter. Return to oven.
3 Increase heat to 400°F (200°C), Gas 6. Roast a further 20 minutes or until golden brown.
  Remove to warm serving dish, sprinkle with chopped nuts and parsley, and keep hot.
4 Stand roasting tin (pan) over moderate heat. Stir in flour. Gradually blend in chicken
  stock. Bring to boil, stirring continuously. Simmer 2 minutes. Blend in sherry. Season.
5 Garnish chicken with lemon and watercress. Serve with the sherry gravy. Accompany
  with sauté potatoes and a salad of crispy fried bacon, grapefruit segments and watercress,
  all tossed in french dressing.

Normandy Cream Chicken with Calvados

(serves 8)

Borrowed from the rich cuisine of Norman France, this showpiece chicken dish has a mellow, indefinable flavour brought about by the addition of calvados— apple brandy 'brewed' in North France and well loved by the locals for drinking and cooking.

8 large joints chicken

salt and pepper to taste

2 garlic cloves, peeled and crushed

4oz (125g) butter, melted ($\frac{1}{2}$ cup)

2 tsp salad oil (3 tsp)

8oz (225g) button mushrooms, trimmed (about $2\frac{1}{2}$ cups)

2oz (50g) flour ($\frac{1}{2}$ cup)

1pt (575ml) sweet cider ($2\frac{1}{2}$ cups apple cider)

$\frac{1}{4}$pt (150ml) double cream ($\frac{5}{8}$ cup heavy cream)

3 tbsp calvados ($4\frac{1}{2}$ tbsp)

1 Place joints in roasting tin, skin sides uppermost. Sprinkle with salt, pepper, garlic and half the butter. Roast 1 hour in oven set to 400°F (200°C), Gas 6.

2 Heat rest of butter in large pan or skillet. Add mushrooms. Fry 5 minutes, turning. Leave on one side temporarily.

3 Remove chicken from oven and transfer to large serving dish. Pour pan juices into saucepan. Stir in flour to form a roux.

4 Blend in cider. Cook, stirring non-stop, until sauce comes to the boil and thickens. Simmer 5 minutes. Whisk in cream. Stir in fried mushrooms.

5 Reheat gently without boiling. Heat calvados to lukewarm in separate pan. Ignite. Add to sauce when flames have subsided. Adjust seasoning to taste. Pour over chicken. Accompany with boiled potatoes.

Kashmir-style Chicken and Poppy-seed Curry

(serves 6)

With oriental overtones, this is a rich, delicate and unusual curry
which can be mild and gentle or as fiery as you like, depending on the
amount of cayenne pepper. It is, I admit, an extravagant but
impressive party dish served with Basmati rice, a dish of cool yogurt
flavoured with fresh chopped mint (or bottled if the fresh is out of season)
and mango chutney. Freshly cooked leaf spinach also blends well with the other
flavours and makes a most companionable accompaniment.

2oz (50g) unsalted butter or ghee ($\frac{1}{4}$ cup)
6 medium-sized chicken joints
2 level tbsp poppy seeds (3 level tbsp)
2 rounded tbsp desiccated coconut (3 rounded tbsp)
4 rounded tbsp ground almonds (6 rounded tbsp)
1 rounded tbsp garam masala ($1\frac{1}{2}$ rounded tbsp)
1 rounded tsp powdered ginger ($1\frac{1}{2}$ rounded tsp)
$\frac{1}{2}$ to 2 level tsp cayenne pepper ($\frac{3}{4}$ to $4\frac{1}{2}$ level tsp)
$\frac{1}{2}$ level tsp saffron strands ($\frac{3}{4}$ level tsp) (optional)
1 level tsp cumin seeds ($1\frac{1}{2}$ level tsp)
1 rounded tsp turmeric ($1\frac{1}{2}$ rounded tsp)
2 to 3 level tsp salt (3 to $4\frac{1}{2}$ level tsp)
1 large garlic clove, peeled and crushed
6 tbsp milk (9 tbsp)
2 level tbsp tomato purée (3 level tbsp tomato paste)
1 tbsp Amaretto di Saronna ($1\frac{1}{2}$ tbsp)
$\frac{1}{2}$pt (275ml) plain yogurt ($1\frac{1}{4}$ cups)

1 Heat butter or ghee in large and heavy-based frying pan or skillet. Add chicken joints.
Fry fairly briskly until well browned. Remove to plate temporarily.
2 Add next 9 ingredients to butter etc in pan. Fry, stirring, for about 5 minutes. Season
with salt. Add rest of ingredients. Bring to boil, stirring all the time.
3 Replace chicken. Cover. Simmer 25 minutes. Turn chicken over. Continue to cook a
further 25 to 35 minutes until tender. Stir occasionally.

Izarra Turkey with Mushrooms and Cucumber

(serves 4)

A surprise element here, with the heady tang of the Izarra liqueur and cooked cucumber to lend its own unmistakable aroma.

4 turkey breast fillets, each 4oz (125g) in weight
3 level tbsp flour (4½ level tbsp)
2oz (50g) butter (¼ cup)
2 tsp salad oil (3 tsp)
1 large onion, peeled and chopped
¼ level tsp dried ginger (same)
1 level tsp dried basil (1½ level tsp)
1 level tsp mustard powder (1½ level tsp)
2 level tsp salt (3 level tsp)
¾ pt(425ml) stock (2 cups)
6oz (175g) trimmed button mushrooms, sliced (about 1½ cups)
8oz (225g) unpeeled cucumber, cut into small dice (about 1¾ to 2 cups)
3 tbsp yellow Izarra (4½ tbsp)

1 Wash and paper-dry turkey. Coat with flour. Heat butter and oil in frying pan. Add turkey. Fry briskly on both sides until golden brown. Remove to plate temporarily.
2 Add onion to rest of butter and oil in pan. Fry gently until pale gold. Stir in ginger, basil, mustard, salt and any leftover flour. Cook 2 minutes, stirring.
3 Gradually blend in stock. Bring to boil, stirring. Replace turkey. Cover. Simmer 20 minutes.
4 Add mushrooms, cucumber and liqueur. Stir in well. Continue to simmer a further 10 minutes. Serve with freshly boiled rice or pasta but no extra vegetables.

Chicken in Wraps

(serves 4)

Chicken in foil retains all its flavour and can be served in its wrap.

4 medium-sized chicken joints
4 large squares greased foil
1oz (25g) butter, melted (⅛ cup)
2 lemons, washed, dried and thinly sliced
1 large onion, peeled and thinly sliced
salt and pepper to taste
4 tbsp dry sherry (6 tbsp)
4 heaped tbsp flaked almonds, browned in a little butter or margarine (6 tbsp)

1 Wash chicken joints and dry on paper towels. Place on centres of foil. Brush with butter.
2 Top with lemon and onion slices then season with salt and pepper. Pour a tablespoon of sherry over each, then fold foil round chicken portions to form parcels.
3 Transfer to baking dish. Bake 1 hour in oven set to 400°F (200°C), Gas 6. Fold back foil and mound with fried almonds. Serve with vegetables to taste.

Chicken with Walnuts

(serves 6)

Serve with pasta shells, Parmesan, and a green salad in mustardy dressing.

3lb (1½kg) oven-ready chicken, defrosted if frozen, and giblets removed
1 rounded tbsp flour (1½ rounded tbsp all-purpose)
2oz (50g) butter (¼ cup)
2 tbsp salad oil (3 tbsp)
3oz (75g) walnuts, ground to same consistency as coffee for percolating (¾ cup)
1 large garlic clove, crushed
1 level tsp salt (1½ level tsp)
¼pt (150ml) dry white wine (⅝ cup)
1 carton (5oz or 142ml) soured cream (⅝ cup cultured soured cream)
1 tbsp cognac (1½ tbsp)

Chicken Crisp with Sherry Gravy, recipe on page 46 (*British Poultry Information Service*)

1 Wash chicken and dry with paper towels. Divide into 6 joints. Coat with flour.
2 Heat butter and oil in large pan. Add chicken, 2 or 3 joints at a time. Fry until golden brown all over.
3 Stir in walnuts, garlic, salt, wine and cream. Bring gently to boil. Lower heat. Cover. Simmer gently 45 minutes.
4 Pour cognac into small pan. Heat to lukewarm. Ignite. Pour over chicken in pan when flames have subsided. Serve straight away.

Korma-style Chicken Curry

(serves 6)

A mild, creamy curry with a hint of oriental fragrance.

2 tbsp salad oil (3 tbsp)
1 large onion, peeled and chopped (about 1 cup)
1 large garlic clove, peeled and chopped
6 chicken joints (about 3lb or 1½kg total weight)
3 to 4 rounded tsp curry powder (4½ to 6 rounded tsp)
1 can (12oz or 350g) peeled tomatoes (about 1½ cups)
5 slightly rounded tbsp yogurt (7½ rounded tbsp)
3 level tsp salt (4½ level tsp)
2 rounded tbsp desiccated coconut (3 rounded tbsp)
1 level tbsp cornflour (1½ level tbsp cornstarch)
5 tbsp cold water (7½ tbsp)
2 tsp anisette or Sambuca Romana
1 tbsp lemon juice

1 Heat oil in large frying pan or skillet. Add onion and garlic. Fry until light gold. Add chicken joints. Fry over fairly brisk heat until golden brown on both sides.
2 Sprinkle with curry powder. Stir in tomatoes, yogurt, salt and coconut. Slowly bring to boil, stirring. Lower heat. Cover. Simmer 40 minutes.
3 Mix cornflour with a little cold water. Stir in rest of water, anisette or Sambuca Romana and lemon juice. Pour into pan over chicken. Cook gently, stirring, until curry liquid comes to boil and thickens. Simmer slowly, uncovered about 5 minutes.
4 Serve with long grain rice, chutney, sliced onion and tomato, sliced banana tossed in lemon juice and extra yogurt seasoned with salt and chopped mint.

Glazed Ham with Orange, recipe on page 81 (*Gales Honey*)

Rum and Rosemary Chicken Pot

(serves 6)

With freshly cooked spaghetti or cascading egg noodles glistening
with melted butter, this chicken speciality tastes distinctly of Italy and
off-the-beaten-track trattorias in favourite holiday sunspots.

1 large chicken, cut into 6 joints
1 tbsp olive oil (1½ tbsp)
2 large onions, peeled and chopped
2 medium-sized garlic cloves, peeled and crushed
1 large can (1lb 12oz or 794g) tomatoes (about 3½ cups)
2 level tsp salt (3 level tsp)
3 tbsp light rum (4½ tbsp)
1 level tsp dried rosemary (1½ level tsp)

1 Wash and paper-dry chicken. Heat oil in large pan which is broad-based rather than tall. Add chicken. Fry over fairly brisk heat until brown on both sides. Remove to plate temporarily.

2 Add onions and garlic to oil in pan. Fry until pale gold. Stir in tomatoes, salt, rum and rosemary. Bring to boil. Replace chicken. Lower heat. Cover. Simmer 1 hour. Serve very hot.

Mustard-glazed Chicken

(serves 4)

Appetising and appealing, this is an inexpensive dish with a gourmet touch.

4 medium-sized chicken joints
1oz (25g) butter, melted (⅛ cup)
2 level tbsp French mustard such as Meaux (3 level tbsp)
1 tbsp vinegar (1½ tbsp)
2 tsp Sambuca Romana (3 tsp)
finely grated peel of 1 small lemon
parsley for garnishing

1 Wash and dry chicken joints. Stand in grill pan, skin sides down. Brush with melted butter. Grill 10 minutes.
2 Turn. Brush with more butter. Grill 10 minutes. Turn again. Grill further 10 minutes. Turn over so that skin is uppermost.
3 Meanwhile, mix mustard with vinegar, Sambuca Romana and lemon peel. Spread over chicken joints. Grill 5 minutes.
4 Serve hot, garnished with parsley and accompanied with sauté potatoes and a green salad.

Sparkling Armagnac Chicken with Artichokes

(*serves 6*)

Rather gorgeous this, with the artichokes adding a note of distinct subtlety to an already unusual dish.

2oz (50g) butter ($\frac{1}{4}$ cup)
2 tsp salad oil (3 tsp)
1 large chicken, cut into 6 joints and washed
2 medium-sized onions, peeled and grated
2 level tbsp flour (3 level tbsp)
$\frac{1}{2}$pt (275ml) sparkling white wine ($1\frac{1}{4}$ cups)
1 can (14oz or 397g) artichoke hearts in brine, drained ($1\frac{3}{4}$ cups)
$\frac{1}{2}$ level tsp dried tarragon ($\frac{3}{4}$ level tsp)
2 level tsp salt (3 level tsp)
4 rounded tbsp blanched and split almonds, toasted (6 rounded tbsp)
3 tbsp Armagnac ($4\frac{1}{2}$ tbsp)

1 Heat butter and oil in pan. Paper-dry chicken. Fry briskly in butter and oil until golden brown. Remove to plate temporarily.
2 Add onions to remaining butter etc in pan. Fry until golden brown. Stir in flour. Gradually blend in wine. Bring to boil, stirring continuously.
3 Quarter artichoke hearts and add to pan with tarragon, salt and almonds. Replace chicken. Cover. Simmer very slowly for 45 minutes to 1 hour or till tender. Stir occasionally.
4 Heat Armagnac to lukewarm. Pour over chicken. Ignite. Serve when flames have subsided.

Thousand Memory Duckling

(serves 4 to 6)

A somewhat anglicised version of a Chinese speciality, with a selection of
stir-fry vegetables to go with it. Serve with either plain boiled rice or
noodles (not both as it's said to be unlucky!), and accompany with condiments
of soy sauce and both hot and mild chilli sauces. Begin the meal with one
of the Chinese soups in the starter section, and end simply by serving fresh
or canned mandarins or lychees with a selection of crisp biscuits.
Traditionally, China tea should be offered throughout the meal.

1 duckling (4lb or 2kg), thawed if frozen, and giblets removed
2 tbsp medium sherry (3 tbsp)
1 tbsp soy sauce (1½ tbsp)
1 large garlic clove, peeled and sliced
4 spring onions, trimmed and chopped (4 scallions)
¼pt (150ml) chicken stock, made from cube and water (⅝ cup)
½ level tsp powdered cinnamon (¾ level tsp)
1 level tsp sugar (1½ level tsp)
1 piece stem ginger in syrup, sliced

1 Place washed duckling into large saucepan. Add all remaining ingredients. Bring to
boil.
2 Reduce heat and cover. Simmer gently for 2 hours, turning from time to time. Remove
from pan and drain thoroughly. Transfer to roasting tin.
3 Roast about 30 to 40 minutes in hot oven set to 450°F (230°C), Gas 8, or until duck is
golden brown. To serve, cut into strips and eat with the stir-fry vegetables below and
other recommended accompaniments.

Stir-fry Sherry Vegetables

(serves 4 to 6)

8oz (225g) aubergine, trimmed (1 medium egg plant)
8oz (225g) Florence fennel, trimmed (1 large or 2 medium)
8oz (225g) onions, peeled (2 large)
4oz (125g) button mushrooms, trimmed (1 to 1¼ cups)

56

2 tbsp corn oil (3 tbsp)
1 level tbsp cornflour (1½ level tbsp cornstarch)
2 tbsp bottled oyster sauce (3 tbsp)
1 tbsp medium sherry (1½ tbsp)
2 tbsp soy sauce (3 tbsp)
1 tsp sesame oil (optional)
pinch of sugar

1 Wash and dry vegetables. Cut all into *small* dice of even size. Heat oil in large pan. Add vegetables. Fry briskly for about 4 minutes, turning frequently.
2 Sprinkle with cornflour (cornstarch). Toss well with vegetables. Add rest of ingredients. Bring to boil, stirring all the time. Serve straight away.

Note Vegetables should be fairly crisp, hence small dice and rapid cooking time.

Coolie Pepper Fry

(*serves 4 to 6*)

2 large peppers, yellow for preference (sweet yellow peppers)
2 medium-sized onions, peeled
2 tbsp corn oil (3 tbsp)
1 rounded tbsp cornflour (1½ rounded tbsp cornstarch)
¾pt (425ml) water (1½ cups)
1 chicken stock cube (bouillon cube)
1 level tsp salt (1½ level tsp)
2 tbsp Galliano (3 tbsp)
1 tsp soy sauce (1½ tsp)

1 Wash and dry peppers. Halve. Remove inside seeds. Cut flesh into thin strips.
2 Cut onions into very thin slices. Separate into rings. Heat oil in large pan. Add peppers and onions. Fry briskly until they just begin to turn golden.
3 Stir in cornflour. Mix well. Gradually add water. Crumble in stock or bouillon cube. Bring to boil, stirring continuously.
4 Add salt, Galliano and soy sauce. Toss gently round in pan. Heat through briefly. Serve straight away.

Piquant Duck in Red Wine Sauce

(serves 8)

Knowing the problems associated with carving cooked duck, I tend to cheat and portion the birds (four portions from each) before roasting. This saves serving–time hassle and cooking time. The full-flavoured sauce accompanying the ducks is a bit unusual and worth trying.

2 large ducks, each cut into 4 portions

2oz (50g) flour ($\frac{1}{2}$ cup all-purpose)

1pt (575ml) dry red wine ($2\frac{1}{2}$ cups)

3 rounded tbsp tomato purée ($4\frac{1}{2}$ rounded tbsp tomato paste)

1 level tsp garlic salt ($1\frac{1}{2}$ level tsp)

$\frac{1}{2}$ level tsp dried thyme (same)

1 level tbsp sugar ($1\frac{1}{2}$ level tbsp)

2 tsp Worcestershire sauce (3 tsp)

2 rounded tsp French mustard (3 rounded tsp)

4 tbsp water (6 tbsp)

2 tbsp Grand Marnier (3 tbsp)

salt and pepper to taste

Garnish
canned mandarins, drained
watercress

1 Arrange duck portions, in single layer, in large roasting tin, with skin sides uppermost. Pick with fork to allow fat to run freely.
2 Roast $1\frac{1}{4}$ hours in oven set to 400°F (200°C), Gas 6. Remove from tin and arrange on large, warm serving platter. Keep hot.
3 To make sauce, pour off all but 3 tbsp ($4\frac{1}{2}$ tbsp) duckling fat from roasting tin. Transfer to saucepan. Stir in flour to form roux. Cook 2 minutes without browning.
4 Gradually blend in red wine and tomato purée. Cook, stirring, until mixture comes to boil and thickens. Add all remaining ingredients.
5 Heat through until hot. Pour over duck portions. Garnish with a border of mandarins and watercress.

Roast Goose with Savoury Rice Dressing

(serves 8 to 10)

Try this for Christmas instead of the more usual turkey. The rice dressing
adds a note of originality to a rather special dish.

1 goose (oven-ready) weighing about 10lb or $5\frac{1}{2}$kg

2 large onions, peeled

4oz (100g) butter ($\frac{1}{2}$ cup)

1lb (450g) apples, peeled and sliced (2 large)

8oz (225g) extra onions, peeled and chopped (about $2\frac{1}{2}$ cups)

4 medium-sized celery stalks, scrubbed and chopped (about 1 to $1\frac{1}{4}$ cups)

1 small green pepper, de-seeded and chopped (sweet green pepper)

12oz (350g) American long grain rice (about 2 cups)

1pt (575ml) chicken stock ($2\frac{1}{2}$ cups)

$\frac{1}{4}$pt (275ml) dry cider ($\frac{5}{8}$ cup)

$\frac{1}{4}$ level tsp mixed spice

salt and pepper to taste

2 tbsp Drambuie

green peas for serving

parsley for garnishing

1 Remove giblet bag from goose. Wash bird under cold, running water. Dry inside and
out with paper towels. Place whole onions inside body cavity.
2 Stand goose on wire grid in roasting tin. Prick skin all over. Sprinkle with salt for extra
crispness. Roast $3\frac{1}{2}$ hours in oven set to 350°F (180°C), Gas 4.
3 About 45 minutes before goose is ready, heat butter in pan. Add apples and prepared
vegetables. Fry 10 minutes or until pale gold. Stir in rest of ingredients, except for
Drambuie. Bring to boil. Stir round.
4 Lower heat. Cover. Simmer 15 to 20 minutes or until rice grains are tender and have
absorbed all the liquid.
5 Make usual gravy with pan juices (first pouring off most of the fat) and flavour with
Drambuie. Serve with the goose, along with the rice and peas. Garnish with parsley.

Cranberry Venison with Mandarin Sauce

(*serves 8 to 10*)

Bearing in mind that some people have access to venison, I felt bound
to include a recipe for this lean and tender meat which works out no more
expensive than a joint of roasting beef. Haunch is the best cut of all,
but my Hertfordshire butcher is a dab hand with more economical shoulder,
which he rolls expertly and wraps in beef fat to keep the meat moist and
succulent. Invest in venison if the opportunity presents itself and serve
it with my 'Compromise' sauce, based on a can of condensed soup.

1 piece rolled shoulder of venison weighing 3¼lb (1½kg)

Sauce
1 can condensed oxtail soup
2 tbsp mandarin liqueur (3 tbsp)
5 tbsp water (7½ tbsp)
1 rounded tbsp cranberry sauce (1½ rounded tbsp)
2 rounded tsp Bordeaux mustard (3 rounded tsp)
2 tbsp lemon juice (3 tbsp)
1 tbsp double cream (1½ tbsp heavy cream)

1 If venison has been in the refrigerator, bring back to kitchen temperature before
washing and drying with paper towels.
2 To roast, stand on grid in baking tin. Place in oven preheated to 450°F (230°C), Gas 8.
Reduce temperature to 300°F (160°C), Gas 3. Continue to roast, allowing 45 minutes
per 16 oz (450g) and 30 minutes over. Baste from time to time.
3 Remove from oven. Lift venison on to carving board. Drain off fat from roasting tin
(which may be kept and used later as dripping), leaving behind, if possible, some of the
meat juices.
4 Stand roasting tin over low heat. Add soup and all remaining sauce ingredients. Stir
continuously until mixture comes to a slow boil and bubbles gently. Cook 5 minutes.
5 Carve venison thinly and accompany with well drained canned pear halves filled with
extra cranberry sauce, butter fried mushrooms and small boiled potatoes tossed in
butter. Pass the sauce separately.

Apple Duck with Drambuie Sauce

(serves 4)

In place of the more customary orange sauce with roast duck, I have developed an apple purée sauce which glows with aromatic Drambuie, a trace of garlic and French or German mustard.

1 x 4lb (2kg) duck
salt

Sauce
1 level tbsp flour (1½ level tbsp all-purpose)
¼pt (150ml) water ($\frac{5}{8}$ cup)
5 rounded tbsp sweetened apple purée (7½ rounded tbsp)
½ level tsp salt ($\frac{3}{4}$ level tsp)
1 tbsp Drambuie (1½ tbsp)
1 level tsp French or German mustard (1½ level tsp)
½ level tsp garlic granules ($\frac{3}{4}$ level tsp)

1 Wash and paper-dry duck. Prick all over with a fork. Sprinkle with salt. Stand on rack. Place in roasting tin (pan). Roast 2 hours at 400°F (200°C), Gas 6.
2 Remove from oven. Stand on carving board and keep hot. To make sauce, pour off all but 2 tbsp fat (3 tbsp) from tin (pan) then stand tin over low heat.
3 Stir in flour to form roux. Gradually blend in water. Cook, stirring continually, until mixture comes to boil and thickens. Stir in purée, salt, Drambuie, mustard and garlic granules.
4 Reheat till bubbling, stirring. Portion duck and serve with the apple sauce. Accompany with roast potatoes and a mixed salad or vegetables to taste.

Mustardy Rabbit in Cointreau Sauce

(serves 6)

A highly sophisticated French-style dish, which teams superbly with tiny boiled potatoes and elegantly slim green beans tossed in butter.

2oz (50g) butter or margarine ($\frac{1}{4}$ cup)

2 tsp salad oil (1$\frac{1}{2}$ tsp)

4lb (2kg) rabbit joints

2 level tbsp cornflour (3 level tbsp cornstarch)

$\frac{1}{2}$pt (275ml) chicken stock (1$\frac{1}{4}$ cups bouillon)

$\frac{1}{2}$pt (275ml) milk (1$\frac{1}{4}$ cups)

2 rounded tsp French or German mustard (3 rounded tsp)

2 tbsp lemon juice (3 tbsp)

2 tbsp Cointreau (3 tbsp)

1 level tsp dried basil (1$\frac{1}{2}$ level tsp)

2 level tsp salt (3 level tsp)

1 Heat butter and oil in large, heavy frying pan or skillet. Add rabbit joints. Fry briskly until brown all over. Remove to plate temporarily.

2 Add cornflour (cornstarch) to butter or margarine and oil in pan to form a roux. Cook 1 minute over low heat.

3 Gradually blend in stock and milk. Cook, stirring, until sauce comes to the boil and thickens. Whisk in mustard, lemon juice, Cointreau and basil. Season with salt. Mix well.

4 Replace rabbit. Cook 5 minutes. Turn over. Cover pan. Simmer 35 to 45 minutes or until tender. Serve with suggested accompaniments.

Hazlenut Rum Beefburgers

(serves 4)

An uncomplicated recipe which is packed with crunch and flavour. Keep for mid-week eating and serve with baked jacket potatoes and grilled tomatoes.

1lb (450g) lean minced beef (16oz ground beef)
1 medium-sized onion, peeled and grated
1 level tsp salt (1½ level tsp)
1 medium-sized egg, lightly beaten
1 tbsp navy rum (1½ tbsp)
2 heaped tbsp hazelnuts, chopped (3 heaped tbsp)
1oz (25g) butter or margarine for frying (⅛ cup)

1 Mix beef thoroughly with onion, salt, egg, rum and hazelnuts. With damp hands, shape into 8 thickish beefburgers.
2 Heat butter or margarine in frying pan. Add beefburgers. Fry very gently for 25 to 30 minutes, turning twice.

Pheasant in the Pot

(serves 8)

A splendid affair fit for discerning friends of impeccable taste!

2 tbsp salad oil (3 tbsp)
1 large onion, peeled and chopped (about 1 cup)
1 large garlic clove, peeled and chopped
1 brace of pheasant (2 pheasant with total weight of about 4lb or 2kg)
½pt (275ml) dry red wine (1¼ cups)
3 level tsp salt (4½ level tsp)
1 bouquet garni bag
2 level tbsp cornflour (3 level tbsp cornstarch)
2 tbsp Cointreau or Grand Marnier
2 level tbsp redcurrant jelly (3 tbsp)

1 Heat oil in large casserole pot. Add onion and garlic. Fry over low heat until pale gold, about 12 to 15 minutes.
2 Meanwhile, skin pheasant and cut each bird into 4 joints. Add to pan, a few pieces at a time. Fry until golden brown. Repeat until all the pheasant has been fried and is in the casserole.
3 Add wine, salt and bouquet garni bag. Bring to boil, stirring. Lower heat. Cover. Simmer gently 45 minutes. Remove bouquet garni bag.
4 Mix cornflour (cornstarch) smoothly with Cointreau or Grand Marnier. Add to pheasant with redcurrant jelly. Boil gently, stirring, until liquid thickens and jelly melts.
5 Simmer a further 5 minutes. Serve with boiled potatoes and seasonal green vegetables.

Boeuf en Croûte

(serves 8)

One of the glories of the French kitchen, Boeuf en Croûte—beef in a crust—is one of the greatest luxuries of all time and must be made with top quality ingredients, irrespective of cost. Therefore, consider this one only when you are feeling very rich or have something extra special to celebrate.

1½lb (675g) beef fillet in one piece
1oz (25g) butter, melted (⅛ cup)
6oz (175g) smooth liver pâté (same)
2 tbsp brandy or cognac (3 tbsp)
1 large packet (13oz or 370g) frozen puff pastry, thawed
beaten egg for brushing

1 Stand fillet in roasting tin and brush with butter. Roast 15 minutes at 425°F (220°C), Gas 7. Remove from oven. Cool completely.
2 Beat liver pâté and alcohol smoothly together. Spread over top and sides of meat.
3 Cut pastry into 2 pieces, one a little larger than the other. Roll out the smaller piece into a rectangle measuring 9 x 7½in (22·5 x 18·75cm).
4 Stand meat centrally on top. Brush pastry edges with water. Roll out second piece of pastry about 1in (2·5cm) larger all the way round than the first piece.
5 Use to cover meat, pressing pastry edges well together to seal. Prick top in 2 places with a fork. Stand on ungreased and dampened baking tray. Brush with beaten egg.
6 Bake 20 minutes at 425°F (220°C), Gas 7. Reduce temperature to 350°F (180°C), Gas 4 and bake a further 20 minutes. Cut into slices and serve with Rich Brown Sauce and vegetables to taste.

Rich Brown Sauce

2oz (50g) butter or margarine (¼ cup)
2 tsp salad oil (3 tsp)
1 medium-sized onion, peeled and chopped
1 medium-sized carrot, peeled and grated
1 large celery stalk, coarsely chopped
a handful of parsley
3 level tbsp flour (4½ level tbsp)
¾pt (425ml) beef stock (2 cups)
2 level tbsp tomato purée (3 level tbsp tomato paste)
1 bouquet garni bag

salt and pepper to taste
1 tbsp tawny port or medium sherry (1½ tbsp)

1 Heat butter or margarine and oil in heavy saucepan. Add onion, carrot, celery and parsley. Fry gently until golden brown, allowing about 10 to 15 minutes.
2 Stir in flour to form roux. Fry over low heat for 5 minutes or until flour turns a dark biscuity colour.
3 Gradually blend in beef stock. Cook, stirring, until sauce comes to the boil and thickens. Lower heat.
4 Add tomato purée, bouquet garni bag and salt and pepper to taste. Cover. Simmer over minimal heat for 45 minutes. Stir occasionally. Remove bouquet garni bag.
5 For thickish sauce, purée all ingredients together in blender goblet. Alternatively, strain sauce and discard vegetables etc. In either case, reheat until hot then stir in port or sherry.

Remarkable Beef Braise

(serves 6)

A top-drawer beef dish, enhanced by the unusual combination of courgettes, chestnuts and Dubonnet. Serve it with Cider Potatoes which are closely related to one of my favourite classics—Potatoes Savoyard.

2 tbsp salad oil (3 tbsp)
2½lb (just over 1kg) braising steak, in one piece
1lb (450g) washed courgettes, unpeeled and sliced (about 3½ cups)
1 large garlic clove, peeled and crushed
1 can (15½oz or 440g) whole chestnuts in water (2 cups) or alternatively use
8oz (225g) cooked chestnuts (about 1½ cups)
1 to 2 level tsp salt (1½ to 3 level tsp)
¼pt (160ml) Dubonnet (⅝ cup)
1 level tsp dried thyme (1½ level tsp)

1 Heat oil in large pan. Add washed and dried steak. Fry on all sides until golden brown. Remove to plate temporarily.
2 Add courgettes and garlic to remaining oil in tin. Fry 10 minutes. Stir in chestnuts (drained if canned), salt, Dubonnet and thyme.
3 Bring to boil, stirring. Add steak. Lower heat. Cover. Simmer about 2 to 2½ hours or until meat is tender. Remove from pan.
4 Carve into slices. Serve with vegetables etc from pan and the potato dish overleaf.

Cider Potatoes

(serves 6 generously)

An outstanding accompaniment to most meat and poultry dishes, and also satisfying as a main dish in its own right served with mixed salad or cooked fresh vegetables to taste.

3lb (1½kg) peeled potatoes, washed and cut into hair-thin slices (a food processor is useful for this)
6oz (175g) Cheddar cheese, grated (1½ cups)
3oz (75g) butter or margarine, melted (⅜ cup)
2 garlic cloves, peeled and crushed
1½ level tsp salt (same)
¾pt (425ml) cider (2 cups)

1 Dry potatoes thoroughly in clean tea towel. Arrange half over base of well buttered, shallow heatproof dish measuring about 10in (22·5cm) in diameter.
2 Sprinkle with half the cheese, half the butter or margarine and all the garlic. Season with half the salt.
3 Cover with rest of potatoes then sprinkle with remaining cheese, butter or margarine and salt. Pour cider gently into dish over potatoes.
4 Bake, uncovered, 1¾ hours at 350°F (180°C), Gas 4, when top should be golden brown and crusty-looking. Spoon out of dish to serve.

Beef Tokańy

(serves 6)

One of the glories of the Hungarian kitchen, Beef Tokańy is as colourful and vivacious as the people themselves, and should be accompanied with a full-blown red wine such as Bull's Blood. The most apt accompaniments are small pasta shells or freshly boiled potatoes.

2 tbsp lard or salad oil (3 tbsp shortening or oil)
3 large onions, peeled and finely chopped
1½lb (700 to 750g) braising steak, cut into small cubes
1 level tbsp paprika (1½ tbsp sweet paprika)
3 tsp anisette (4½ tsp)
1 large green pepper, washed, de-seeded and cut into strips

66

4 large tomatoes, blanched, skinned and chopped

2 level tsp salt (3 level tsp)

4oz (125g) mushrooms, trimmed and sliced

1 carton (5fl oz or 142ml) soured cream ($\frac{5}{8}$ cup cultured soured cream)

1 Heat lard or salad oil in large pan. Add onions. Fry slowly until golden brown. Keep lid on pan and allow 15 minutes covered and about 10 minutes uncovered.
2 Increase heat. Add beef, a few cubes at a time. Fry until well browned. Continue until all the beef has been added.
3 Stir in paprika, anisette, green pepper, tomatoes and salt. Bring to boil, stirring. Lower heat. Cover. Simmer very slowly for 1$\frac{1}{2}$ hours, during which time the ingredients will form their own sauce without the addition of water. Stir occasionally.
4 Add mushrooms and mix in well. Cook 10 minutes. Stir in soured cream. Serve with suggested accompaniments.

Mozzarella Mince

(serves 4 to 6)

A cross between Spaghetti Bolognese and Lasagne! Here is a
convenient dish which can be made with reasonable speed
from the sort of ingredients one is likely to have in
the store cupboard and refrigerator.

1lb (450g) lean minced beef (16oz ground beef)

1 large garlic clove, crushed

$\frac{1}{2}$ to 1 level tsp salt

8oz (225g) cooked pasta shapes, weight *after* cooking (about 4 cups)

2 tbsp sweet martini

1 can (14oz or 397g) tomatoes (about 2 cups)

3oz (75g) mushrooms, trimmed and sliced (about 1 cup)

8oz (225g) pack Mozzarella cheese, sliced

2 rounded tbsp grated Parmesan cheese

1 Spread beef over base of non-stick pan and fry until brown and crumbly, stirring with a wooden fork or spoon to break up the meat. Allow about 15 minutes.
2 Add garlic, salt, pasta, martini, tomatoes and mushrooms. Crush tomatoes with fork or spoon then bring mixture just up to boil. Cover. Simmer 10 minutes.
3 Transfer to greased dish, top with Mozzarella cheese then sprinkle with Parmesan cheese. Glaze under hot grill. Serve straight away with salad or fried courgettes (zucchini).

Exotic Coffee Beef

(serves 4 to 6)

A curious blend of flavours are woven together to interesting effect in this fragrant beef dish enhanced with coffee liqueur and spices. The sauce thickens by itself.

2oz (50g) butter or margarine ($\frac{1}{4}$ cup)
1 large onion, peeled and chopped
2lb (900g) lean stewing beef, cut into small cubes
$\frac{1}{4}$pt (150ml) water ($\frac{5}{8}$ cup)
2 rounded tbsp tomato purée (3 rounded tbsp tomato paste)
3 tbsp coffee liqueur such as Tia Maria or Kahlua ($4\frac{1}{2}$ tbsp)
1 level tsp salt ($1\frac{1}{2}$ level tsp)
$\frac{1}{2}$ level tsp powdered ginger ($\frac{3}{4}$ level tsp)
$\frac{1}{4}$ level tsp grated nutmeg (same)
8oz (225g) button mushrooms, trimmed and thinly sliced (about $2\frac{1}{2}$ cups)
2 tbsp lemon juice (3 tbsp)

1 Heat butter or margarine in large pan. Add onion. Fry gently until pale gold. Add meat cubes, a few pieces at a time.
2 Fry briskly until well sealed and brown. Pour water into pan over meat. Add purée, coffee liqueur, salt, ginger and nutmeg.
3 Bring to boil, stirring. Lower heat. Cover. Simmer $1\frac{1}{2}$ to 2 hours or until meat is tender.
4 Add mushrooms and lemon juice. Continue to cook, covered, an extra 15 minutes. Serve with boiled potatoes and green vegetables to taste.

Mexican-style Meat Loaf

(serves 8)

A stunning main course, ideal for economical entertaining.

$1\frac{1}{2}$lb (675g) raw minced beef ($1\frac{1}{2}$lb ground beef)
3oz (75g) fresh white breadcrumbs ($1\frac{1}{2}$ cups)
2 medium-sized eggs, beaten

4 heaped tsp creamed horseradish sauce (6 heaped tsp)
5oz (150g) Florence fennel (1 medium bulb)
3oz (75g) green pepper (1 small sweet green pepper)
8oz (225g) onion (2 large)
2 tbsp tequila (3 tbsp)
2 level tsp salt (3 level tsp)
2 rounded tbsp mayonnaise (3 rounded tbsp)
2oz (50g) strong cheese, finely grated ($\frac{1}{2}$ cup)

1 Combine beef with crumbs, eggs and horseradish sauce.
2 Trim fennel. Halve pepper and de-seed. Peel onions and cut each into quarters. Pass through mincer or mince fairly finely in food processor or electric grinder.
3 Add to meat mixture with tequila and salt. Mix well. Shape into a 10 x 6 x 1$\frac{1}{2}$in (25 x 15 x 3·75cm) loaf on foil-lined baking tray (cookie sheet), first brushed with melted margarine or oil.
4 Bake 45 minutes in oven preheated to 350°F (180°C), Gas 4. Remove from oven. Spread top with mayonnaise and sprinkle with cheese.
5 Return to hot oven set to 425°F (220°C), Gas 7. Cook a further 15 to 20 minutes or until golden brown. Slice and serve hot with sauté potatoes and vegetables to taste, or jacket potatoes and a green salad.

Dreamers Lunch Punch

(serves 4 to 6)

A foamy, lighthearted meal-in-a-glass makes perfect hot weather 'eating', and this particular brew is packed with vitamins, flavour and sparkle.

3 medium-sized oranges
1 medium-sized, ripe avocado
3 tbsp mead (4 tbsp)
1$\frac{1}{4}$pt (725ml) chilled milk (3 cups)
mint sprigs

1 Wash and dry 1 orange. Cut into slices and reserve for decoration.
2 Grate off peel and squeeze juice of remaining two oranges. Peel avocado as you would peel a pear, starting from the pointed end.
3 Dice flesh (discarding stone). Place in blender goblet with orange peel and juice, mead and about one-third of the milk.
4 Blend until mixture is smooth and foamy. Transfer to large jug. Whisk in rest of milk.
5 Pour into glasses, decorate each with an orange slice and mint sprig. Drink immediately.

Artichokes 'Farci' from the Dordogne

(serves 4)

I am very grateful to young Marielle who, at the request of
an old friend of our family, her aunt, came to cook for us
and 'do' for us one wet and miserable summer. We spent
all our spare time concocting gargantuan meals and dwelling
on the complexities of the English language in general, and
irregular verbs in particular. Marielle's mother, Francine,
is a fully-trained butcher and ex-restaurateur, and is presently
employed to cook for the owners of a private château in the
Dordogne region of France. Having travelled and worked throughout
the country, she is immensely talented in preparing French
regional dishes and so, as it turned out, is her daughter.
Hence this mouth-watering recipe for stuffed artichokes which
we adapted slightly from an old French recipe book—Marielle's
bible for the few weeks she was with us and eventually one of
my most interesting instruction manuals.

4 large globe artichokes
boiling salted water
1lb (450g) raw minced beef (16oz ground beef)
1 large onion, peeled and chopped ($\frac{3}{4}$ to 1 cup)
1 medium-sized egg, beaten
2 tbsp milk (3 tbsp)
2 heaped tbsp finely chopped parsley (3 heaped tbsp)
pepper to taste

Sauce
2 tbsp olive oil (3 tbsp)
2 large garlic cloves, peeled and crushed
1 can (about 14oz or 398g) tomatoes ($1\frac{3}{4}$ cups)
2 tbsp brandy (3 tbsp)
1 level tsp each salt and sugar

1 Break stem off each artichoke and remove first two layers of leaves as these are usually
tough.

2 Wash by soaking for 30 minutes in cold, salted water. Drain by shaking.

3 Place upright in large pan. One-third fill with boiling water. Add 1 level tsp salt. Cover. Boil fairly gently about 45 minutes to 1 hour or until tender. To test, pull out one or two leaves, with hand protected by oven glove: if they move easily, the artichokes are cooked.

4 Drain thoroughly by standing upside-down in large colander. Leave until completely cold. Place upright. Open out leaves gently and remove centre cone.

5 You will then come to the 'choke' which looks like a layer of bristles. Pinch these out between forefinger and thumb, leaving artichoke heart encircled by outside leaves. Leave artichokes on one side temporarily.

6 To make stuffing, fry meat in heavy-based pan, without additional fat, until dry and crumbly. Add onion.

7 Increase heat slightly and fry about 10 minutes or until onions begin to soften slightly. Stir fairly frequently.

8 Stir in all remaining ingredients. Fork-mix until well combined. Remove pan from heat. Spoon equal amounts of stuffing into artichoke hollows.

9 To make sauce, heat oil in wide-based and fairly deep pan. Add garlic. Fry until golden. Stir in tomatoes, breaking down whole ones by mashing coarsely with a fork.

10 Stir in brandy, salt and sugar. Add artichokes to pan, placing them in an upright position. Baste with tomato mixture.

11 Bring gently to boil. Cook gently 45 minutes. Transfer to individual hot plates. Coat with tomato mixture.

12 To eat, pull off outside leaves, dip their fleshy ends in sauce and pass them through your teeth; then discard them. Finally eat stuffing, artichoke heart and sauce all together.

Amaretto Lamb

(*serves 8*)

Lamb with a difference—fragrant with garlic and the distinctive Amaretto di Saronno, and very Italian.

4lb (2kg) leg of lamb
2 garlic cloves, peeled
2 level tbsp cornflour (3 level tbsp cornstarch)
½pt (275ml) water (1¼ cups)
2 tbsp Amaretto di Saronno (3 tbsp)
1 level tsp French mustard (1½ level tsp)
salt and pepper to taste
½ level tsp dried thyme (¾ level tsp)

1 Cut nicks in lamb flesh with pointed knife then insert garlic, cut into slivers. Transfer to roasting tin (pan). Place in oven set to 425°F (220°C), Gas 7. Reduce temperature to 375°F (190°C), Gas 5.
2 Roast 2 hours. Remove lamb from tin (pan) and place on carving board. Keep warm.
3 Pour off and discard all but 2 tbsp (3 tbsp) fat from roasting tin (pan). Stand over low heat. Stir in cornflour. Cook 2 minutes.
4 Gradually blend in rest of ingredients. Cook, stirring, until sauce comes to boil and thickens. Simmer 5 minutes.
5 To serve, carve lamb as desired and serve with the sauce. Accompany with baby new potatoes and the Pernod Cabbage below.

Pernod Cabbage

(*serves 8*)

Amazingly tasty and a unique way of presenting cabbage.

1 cabbage weighing about 2 to 2½lb (about 1kg)
½pt (275ml) boiling stock (1¼ cups)
1 level tsp salt (1½ level tsp)
4 tsp Pernod (6 tsp)

1 Remove bruised outer leaves from cabbage then cut head into 8 wedges.
2 Stand in large frying pan or skillet. Mix rest of ingredients together. Pour over cabbage. Bring to boil over medium heat.

3 Lower heat. Cover. Cook gently about 20 minutes or until cabbage is tender but still crisp.

Lamb Cutlets à la Domecq

(serves 4)

Sherried lamb fillets, topped with pats of aromatic rum butter, make a novel main course with sauté potatoes and aubergine slices.

Savoury Rum Butter (which should be made the day before)
2oz (50g) unsalted butter ($\frac{1}{4}$ cup)
3 tsp navy rum ($4\frac{1}{2}$ tsp)
$\frac{1}{2}$ level tsp garlic salt ($\frac{3}{4}$ level tsp)
$\frac{1}{2}$ level tsp dried tarragon ($\frac{3}{4}$ level tsp)
2 level tsp French mustard (3 level tsp)

4 leg of lamb fillets, each 8oz (225g) in weight
2 rounded tbsp flour, well seasoned with salt and pepper (3 rounded tbsp all-purpose)
2oz (50g) butter ($\frac{1}{4}$ cup)
1 tbsp salad oil ($1\frac{1}{2}$ tbsp)
1 medium-sized garlic clove, peeled and crushed
4 tbsp dry Oloroso sherry (6 tbsp)

Garnish
grilled tomato halves
wedges of lemon

1 To make Savoury Rum Butter, cream butter until very soft and pale in colour. Beat in all remaining ingredients. Shape into a small roll on a piece of foil. Wrap and refrigerate. Cut into thick slices for using.
2 Wash and paper-dry lamb. Coat with flour. Heat butter and oil in large frying pan or skillet. Add garlic. Fry 2 minutes.
3 Add lamb fillets. Fry 10 minutes, turning twice. Remove to 4 warm plates. Keep hot. Add sherry to pan juices. Swish round. Bring to boil. Pour over fillets.
4 Top with pats of Savoury Rum Butter then garnish with tomatoes and lemon. Serve straight away.

Curried Lamb from Uttar Pradesh

(serves 8)

Found in a cook book sent to me by some contacts in India, I have adapted one
of the recipes to produce this eminently tasty lamb dish using the least
expensive cut.

3oz (75g) butter or ghee ($\frac{3}{8}$ cup)

4lb (2kg) neck of lamb, chopped-up into 3in (7·5cm) pieces (same), fat trimmed

3 large onions, peeled and chopped

3 large garlic cloves, peeled and crushed

6 cardamoms, crushed

4 cloves

2in (5cm) piece of cinnamon stick

2 rounded tsp cumin seeds (3 rounded tsp)

$\frac{1}{4}$ level tsp ground nutmeg (same)

1 level tsp turmeric (1$\frac{1}{2}$ level tsp)

1 level tsp ground coriander (1$\frac{1}{2}$ level tsp)

1 level tsp fenugreek (1$\frac{1}{2}$ level tsp)

3 rounded tsp curry powder (4$\frac{1}{2}$ rounded tsp)

1 rounded tsp powdered ginger (1$\frac{1}{2}$ rounded tsp)

4 tbsp water (6 tbsp)

1 tbsp anisette

1 tbsp fresh lemon or lime juice (1$\frac{1}{2}$ tbsp)

$\frac{3}{4}$pt (425ml) natural yogurt (2 cups)

2 to 3 level tsp salt (3 to 4$\frac{1}{2}$ level tsp)

1 Heat butter or ghee in large pan. Add lamb. Fry briskly until well browned. Remove to
  plate temporarily.
2 Add onions and garlic to remaining butter in pan. Fry over medium heat until light
  gold. Stir in cardamoms, cloves, cinnamon, cumin seeds, nutmeg, turmeric, coriander,
  fenugreek, curry powder and ginger.
3 Blend in water, anisette, lemon or lime juice, yogurt and salt. Bring to boil, stirring.
  Replace lamb. Stir until all pieces are well coated with yogurt mixture. Cover.
4 Simmer about 1$\frac{1}{2}$ hours, stirring occasionally. Remove from heat. Cool completely.
  Refrigerate overnight as this improves the flavour of the curry.
5 Remove hard layer of fat from the top before serving. Bring to boil. Bubble gently,
  covered, for 15 minutes. Serve with boiled rice, assorted chutneys and a dish of fried
  coconut for sprinkling over each portion.

74

M'lord's Lamb and Lager Roast

(serves 6)

An appetising adventure of a meal, which makes superb cold-weather eating.

3lb (1½kg) leg of lamb (for leanness) or shoulder
flour
1 tbsp margarine, melted (1½ tbsp)
8oz (225g) carrots, peeled and sliced (about 1½ cups)
8oz (225g) celery, well washed and chopped (about 1½ cups)
8oz (225g) potatoes, peeled and diced (about 1½ cups)
4oz (125g) swedes, peeled and diced (about ¾ cup)
1 can (14oz or 400g) tomatoes (about 1¾ cups)
2 tbsp whisky (3 tbsp)
½pt (275ml) lager (1¼ cups)
salt and pepper to taste
2 sprigs fresh rosemary

1 Trim meat of excess fat otherwise the end result will be very greasy. Wash joint and dry with paper towels. Coat all over with flour.
2 Melt margarine in large, flameproof casserole. Add lamb. Fry briskly until golden brown all over. Remove to plate temporarily.
3 Add prepared vegetables to remaining margarine in pan. Fry fairly briskly until pale gold. Add tomatoes, whisky and lager. Bring to boil, stirring.
4 Replace lamb. Season to taste with salt and pepper. Add 1 sprig rosemary. Cover dish with lid or foil.
5 Cook for 2½ to 3 hours in oven set to 350°F (180°C), Gas 4. Uncover. Garnish with second sprig of rosemary.
6 Serve straight from the dish by cutting meat into thick slices and serving with vegetables and cooking liquid. Accompany with extra boiled potatoes and Brussels sprouts.

Marinated Lamb Kebabs

(serves 4)

Classic enough to be Greek, the marinated kebabs are sweet, tender and packed with flavour. Serve them with hollow pitta bread (sometimes spelled pita) and a mixed salad of lettuce, tomatoes, onion, olives and cubes of white cheese—Caerphilly in the absence of the more companionable Greek feta—all tossed together in an olive oil dressing.

1½lb (675g) neck of lamb fillet, trimmed of excess fat

Marinade
¼pt (150ml) dry red wine (⅝ cup)
1 garlic clove, peeled and crushed
1 tbsp brandy (1½ tbsp brandy)
1 level tsp salt (1½ level tsp)
1 level tsp marjoram (1½ level tsp)
½ level tsp coarsely milled black pepper (same)

1 Wash and dry lamb fillet and cut into 2in (5cm) pieces. Transfer to a glass, plastic or enamel dish.
2 Beat all remaining ingredients well together. Pour over lamb. Toss until pieces of meat are coated with wine mixture.
3 Cover and refrigerate overnight. Thread meat onto 4 skewers. Grill under high heat for 15 minutes, turning twice.
4 Meanwhile, strain marinade and boil briskly until 4 tbsp (6tbsp) remain. Pour over kebabs. Serve straight away.

English Chops

(serves 4)

A Pimm's No 1 special with juicy lamb chump chops. Serve this lustrous main course with sauté potatoes and a green salad tossed in French dressing.

1oz (25g) butter (¼ cup)
2 tsp salad oil (3 tsp)
1 large onion, peeled and finely chopped
4 large chump chops

4 level tsp cornflour (6 level tsp cornstarch)
½pt (275ml) Pimm's No 1 (1¼ cups)
1 level tsp salt (1½ level tsp)
¼pt (150ml) water (⅝ cup)

1 Heat butter and oil in large pan. Add onion. Fry gently until golden. Meanwhile wash and paper-dry chops then coat with cornflour (cornstarch).
2 Add to pan. Fry fairly briskly until golden brown on both sides, turning once.
3 Pour Pimm's into pan. Sprinkle with salt. Add water. Bring to boil. Lower heat. Cover. Simmer 20 minutes. Transfer chops to plates and coat with pan juices.

Fruited Lamb Saddle

(serves 8 to 10)

For important occasions, saddle of lamb with a fruity sauce is an impressive sight, partnered elegantly with new potatoes tossed in butter, mange tout, French beans and baby carrots.

1 saddle of lamb weighing about 4lb or 2kg
salt and pepper
1½ level tbsp cornflour (2 level tbsp cornstarch)
½pt (275ml) white grape juice (1¼ cups)
2 tbsp mandarin liqueur (3½ tbsp)
3 rounded tbsp cranberry sauce (4½ tbsp)
1 level tsp onion salt (1½ level tsp)
½ level tsp salt (¾ level tsp)
1 tbsp lemon juice (1½ tbsp)

1 Wash and dry saddle. Sprinkle well with salt and pepper. Place in roasting tin (pan). Roast 15 minutes at 450°F (230°C), Gas 8.
2 Reduce temperature to 350°F (180°C), Gas 4. Roast a further 1¼ hours. Remove to carving board and keep hot.
3 To make sauce, pour away all but 2 tbsp (3 tbsp) fat from roasting tin (pan). Stand tin over low heat. Stir in cornflour.
4 Gradually blend in grape juice, liqueur, cranberry sauce, onion salt, ordinary salt and lemon juice. Cook, stirring, until sauce comes to the boil and thickens. Simmer, whisking, for 5 minutes.
5 Adjust seasoning to taste, pour sauce into dish or boat and pass with the carved saddle.

Gingered Lamb Noisettes

(*serves 4*)

A more unusual way of presenting a favourite cut of lamb, and ideal for the host or hostess without too much spare time.

1 whole loin of lamb, boned
1 garlic clove, peeled and cut
salt and pepper
1oz (25g) butter or margarine ($\frac{1}{8}$ cup)
$\frac{1}{2}$pt (275ml) ginger ale ($1\frac{1}{4}$ cups)
2 tbsp ginger wine (3 tbsp)
2 pieces preserved stem ginger in syrup, cut into strips
1 level tbsp cornflour ($1\frac{1}{2}$ level tbsp cornstarch)
2 tbsp cold water (3 tbsp)

Garnish
potato crisps (chips)
parsley

1 Tie boned lamb at 1in (about 3cm) intervals then cut between the string to form rounds or noisettes. Rub with garlic. Sprinkle with salt and pepper.
2 Melt butter in large frying pan or skillet. Add lamb. Fry fairly briskly on both sides until golden brown. Pour ginger ale and ginger wine into pan.
3 Bring to boil and add ginger strips. Lower heat. Cook gently, uncovered, for about 20 minutes. Turn noisettes over once.
4 Remove lamb to warm serving platter and keep hot. To thicken sauce, mix cornflour (cornstarch) to smooth liquid with water.
5 Add to pan juices. Cook, stirring, until mixture comes to boil and thickens. Adjust seasoning to taste. Pour over lamb. Garnish with potato crisps (chips) and parsley. Serve with fried potato slices and a green salad.

Apple Braised Veal

(*serves 8 generously*)

Remembering that veal can sometimes be bland and also on the dry side, I chanced my luck by cooking a large and elderly leg with a mixture of root vegetables, cider, calvados and bay leaves. When the whole thing had tenderised itself, I stirred soured cream into the pan leftovers and produced what turned out to be a gourmet meal with a mellow, distinguished sauce cossetting moist slices of meat.

1½ tbsp butter or margarine (2 tbsp)

2 tsp salad oil (3 tsp)

1 leg of veal weighing about 4½ lb (2kg)

4 large carrots, peeled and thinly sliced

1 large parsnip, peeled and cut into small cubes

½pt (275ml) dry cider (1¼ cups dry apple cider)

1 level tsp salt (1½ level tsp)

2 small bay leaves

1 level tbsp cornflour (1½ level tbsp cornstarch)

3 tbsp calvados (4½ tbsp)

1 carton (5fl oz or 142ml) soured cream (⅝ cup cultured soured cream)

1 Heat butter or margarine and oil in large saucepan. Add veal (shank end removed). Fry briskly until well browned all over. Remove to plate temporarily.
2 Add carrots and parsnip to rest of butter in pan. Fry 15 minutes or until lightly browned. Stir in cider, salt and bay leaves. Bring to boil.
3 Replace fried veal with shank. Lower heat. Cover. Simmer until very tender, allowing about 2 hours and adding extra cider only if liquid seems to be evaporating too quickly and pan contents appear dry.
4 Remove meat to board. Carve into thick slices. Transfer to warm platter. Keep hot. Mix cornflour smoothly with calvados. Pour into pan. Bring to boil. Cook, stirring, until pan liquid comes to boil and thickens. Whisk in cream.
5 Adjust seasoning to taste. Reheat. Pour over veal. Serve with creamed potatoes (or Snow Potatoes on page 43) and sprouts or quickly cooked cabbage.

Veal Chops Campari

(serves 4)

Glowing pink and immensely appetising,
this is a way of livening up what is often called a dull
and tasteless meat (unless the most
exclusive cut is converted into escalopes and served as
Wiener Schnitzel).

1 tbsp salad oil
12oz (350g) red peppers, de-seeded and cut into strips (2 large red sweet peppers)
2 large garlic cloves, peeled and crushed
4 large veal chops (each about 8oz or 225g), washed and dried with paper towels
3 tbsp Campari (4 tbsp)
1 level tsp salt

1 Heat oil in large and heavy-based frying pan. Add peppers and garlic. Fry over moderate heat until just beginning to turn golden.
2 Move to edges of pan. Add chops, one at a time. Fry until golden on both sides. When all the chops have been fried and are sitting comfortably in the pan, 'baste' with peppers.
3 Pour Campari over chops and sprinkle with salt. Cover. Cook gently for 20 minutes, turning twice. Serve with creamed potatoes and green vegetables.

Brandied Veal Braise with Prunes and Walnuts

(serves 6)

The prunes and nuts do much to enliven the veal, as do the white wine and
vegetables in which the meat is simmered. Serve with fluffy creamed potatoes
and either sprouts or the Pernod Cabbage on page 72.

2oz (50g) butter or margarine ($\frac{1}{4}$ cup)
2 tsp salad oil (3 tsp)
3lb (1$\frac{1}{2}$kg) boned shoulder of veal, tied by butcher into a neat shape
2 level tbsp flour (3 level tbsp all-purpose)
2 large onions, peeled and grated

1 medium-sized carrot, peeled and thinly sliced
½pt (275ml) dry white wine (1¼ cups)
3 heaped tbsp chopped walnuts (4½ heaped tbsp)
1 can (15½oz or 439g) prunes, stoned (2 cups)
2 level tsp salt (3 level tsp)
3 heaped tbsp chopped parsley (4½ heaped tbsp)
2 tbsp brandy (3 tbsp)

1 Heat butter or margarine and oil in large and shallow casserole. Coat veal with flour. Add to pan. Fry briskly until golden brown. Remove to plate. Leave on one side temporarily.
2 Add onions and carrot to remaining fat in pan. Fry until pale gold. Stir in any leftover flour then blend in wine, walnuts, prunes with syrup from can, salt, parsley and brandy.
3 Cook, stirring, until liquid comes to boil. Replace veal, basting top with pan juices. Lower heat. Cover. Simmer very gently for 2 hours. Remove string from veal before carving. Serve with prune and nut sauce from pan, including the vegetables.

Glazed Ham with Orange

(serves about 15)

A highly decorative party dish which tastes as good as it looks. A gladsome thing indeed for Easter festivities, Christmas or New Year galas.

5 to 6lb (2½kg) gammon joint
2 level tbsp French mustard (3 level tbsp)
1 tbsp honey, melted (1½ tbsp)
2 tbsp Grand Marnier or Cointreau (3 tbsp)
4 washed and dried oranges, sliced
Cloves
extra melted honey

1 Place gammon in large pan. Cover with cold water. Bring to boil. Drain. Repeat twice more to remove excess salt.
2 Cover with cold water. Bring slowly to boil. Lower heat. Cover. Simmer gently 3 hours. Drain. Carefully strip off skin.
3 Stand gammon in roasting tin. Brush fat with mustard mixed with honey and Grand Marnier or Cointreau. Bake 20 minutes at 425°F (220°C), Gas 7.
4 Remove from oven. Cover with orange slices and secure with cloves. Brush with extra melted honey. Return to oven. Cook further 15 minutes.
5 Cool completely before carving. Accompany with assorted salads.

Martini Veal with Bacardi

(serves 8)

An undemanding main course which uses one of
the cheaper cuts of meat in a completely new guise.

4lb (2kg) unboned neck of veal
½pt (275ml) dry martini (1¼ cups)
1 large onion, peeled but left whole
1 bouquet garni bag
2 level tsp salt (3 level tsp)
2 level tbsp cornflour (3 level tbsp cornstarch)
2 tbsp water (3 tbsp)
8 heaped tbsp yogurt (12 heaped tbsp)
3 rounded tbsp chopped parsley (4½ rounded tbsp)
1 tbsp Worcestershire sauce (1½ tbsp)
2 tbsp Bacardi (3 tbsp)
1 level tsp marjoram (1½ level tsp)

1 Wash veal. Place in large pan with martini, onion, bouquet garni and salt. Bring to boil. Lower heat. Cover.
2 Simmer very gently for 2 to 2½ hours or until meat is tender. Remove from pan, discarding bouquet garni. Take meat off bones and cut into bite-size pieces.
3 Return pan to low heat. Add cornflour (cornstarch) mixed smoothly with water, yogurt, parsley, Worcestershire sauce, Bacardi and marjoram.
4 Bring to boil, stirring all the time. Replace veal. Cover. Heat through 10 minutes. Serve with creamed potatoes and freshly cooked cabbage.

Marsala Pork with Thyme

(serves 4 to 6)

Pork in party dress makes an appealing change, and this rather pleasant recipe
teams beautifully with Savoury Fried Rice and peas or sprouts.

1oz (25g) butter or margarine (⅛ cup)
1 medium-sized garlic clove, peeled and crushed

1lb (450g) pork fillet, cut into thin slices (like medallions)

4oz (125g) mushrooms and stalks, trimmed and sliced (1 cup)

½ level tsp salt (¾ level tsp)

pepper to taste

½ level tsp dried thyme (¾ level tsp)

4 tbsp marsala (6 tbsp)

3 heaped tbsp double cream (4½ heaped tbsp heavy cream)

2 tbsp lemon juice (3 tbsp)

1 Heat butter or margarine in pan. Add garlic and pork. Fry fairly briskly until golden brown. Reduce heat to medium. Continue to fry 10 minutes, turning from time to time.

2 Add mushrooms. Increase heat. Fry 5 minutes. Season with salt, pepper and thyme. Stir in marsala. Heat through until bubbling.

3 Stir in cream and lemon juice. Adjust seasoning to taste. Accompany with the rice (below) and cooked vegetables to taste.

Savoury Fried Rice

(serves 4 to 6)

1oz (25g) butter of margarine (⅛ cup)

1 medium-sized onion, chopped

1 medium-sized green or red pepper, de-seeded and chopped

8oz (225g) long grain rice (1¼ cups)

1pt (575ml) chicken or beef stock (2½ cups)

1 bay leaf

1 level tsp salt (1½ level tsp)

2 heaped tbsp split and toasted almonds (3 heaped tbsp)

1 Heat butter or margarine in pan. Add onion and pepper. Fry both until pale gold. Stir in rice.

2 Fry further 2 or 3 minutes. Add stock, bay leaf and salt. Bring to boil, fork-stirring continuously.

3 Lower heat. Cover. Cook over medium heat for 20 minutes or until rice grains have absorbed all the liquid and are separate and fluffy.

4 Fork in almonds and serve hot.

Apricot Pork Normandy

(serves 8)

Heady with cider and calvados, this is a beauty of a dish
for any time of year. Serve it with whipped-up potatoes
and buttered green beans tossed with crunchy nuts.

3lb (1¼kg) pork fillets (tenderloin), all fat removed
7oz (200g) dried apricots (about 1¼ cups)
8 fairly thin slices cooked ham, each cut in half
2oz (50g) flour (½ cup all-purpose)
3oz (75g) butter or margarine (¼ cup)
1lb (450g) trimmed leeks, slit and well washed (about 3 medium)
4 large celery stalks, well washed and sliced (about 1½ cups)
8oz (225g) carrots, peeled and diced (about 1½ cups)
1pt (575ml) dry cider (2½ cups apple cider)
4 rounded tbsp tomato purée (6 tbsp tomato paste)
2tbsp Worcestershire sauce (3 tbsp)
salt and pepper to taste
3 tbsp calvados (4½ tbsp)

1 Wash each fillet and dry with paper towels. Slit each lengthwise to form a pocket and
  pack with well washed apricots.
2 Cut into total of 16 portions. Wrap a piece of cooked ham round each. Tie with string
  to hold in place. Coat each heavily with flour.
3 Heat butter or margarine in large and sturdy saucepan. Add portions of meat. Fry
  until golden brown all over. Remove to plate.
4 Add vegetables to remaining butter or margarine in pan. Stir well to mix. Fry gently,
  with lid on pan, for about 30 minutes or until soft and just beginning to turn golden.
5 Replace meat. Sprinkle any leftover flour over the top. Gently pour cider into pan over
  vegetables and meat.
6 Add tomato purée (paste), well blended with Worcestershire sauce. Season. Toss
  gently to mix. Cover. Simmer over minimal heat for 1 to 1½ hours or until meat is
  cooked through and tender.
7 Lift out portions of meat. Remove string. Keep hot. Heat calvados to lukewarm in
  small pan. Ignite. Pour into pan in which meat was cooking. Mix in well.
8 Transfer vegetables and gravy to large serving dish (not too shallow). Top with meat.
  Serve straight away with boiled potatoes and green beans.

Blue Cream Turkey with Port

(serves 4 to 6)

Served with baby pasta and a mixed salad, here is a dish fit
for princes: pieces of cooked turkey nestle together in a
rich sauce made with Stilton cheese and tawny port.

2oz (50g) butter or margarine ($\frac{1}{4}$ cup)
2oz (50g) flour ($\frac{1}{2}$ cup all-purpose)
$\frac{1}{2}$pt (275ml) chicken or turkey stock ($1\frac{1}{4}$ cups)
$\frac{1}{4}$pt (150ml) single cream ($\frac{5}{8}$ cup coffee cream)
$\frac{1}{4}$pt (150ml) milk ($\frac{5}{8}$ cup)
1lb (450g) cold, cooked turkey, diced (about $2\frac{3}{4}$ cups)
4oz (100 to 125g) blue Stilton cheese, crumbled (about 1 to $1\frac{1}{4}$ cups blue cheese)
salt and pepper to taste
2 tbsp tawny port
chopped parsley for garnish

1 Melt butter or maragarine in large saucepan. Stir in flour to form roux. Cook about
1 to 2 minutes without browning.
2 Gradually blend in stock, cream and milk. Cook, stirring continuously, until sauce
comes to the boil and thickens.
3 Add turkey dice. Stir in gently. Bubble over low heat for 15 minutes. Remove from heat.
Add cheese. Leave to stand, covered, 5 minutes.
4 Stir round lightly until cheese melts. Season to taste. Blend in port. Spoon into a warm
serving dish and sprinkle with parsley.

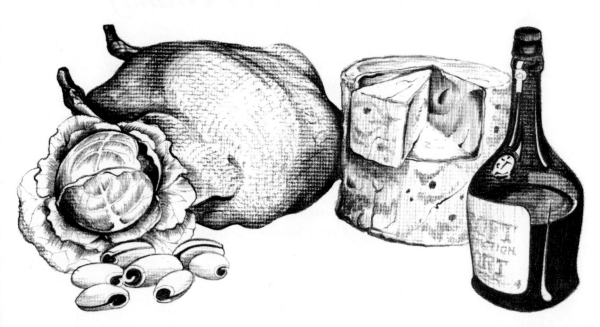

Pork Pâté Loaf

(serves 8)

A reasonably-priced meal that tastes special.
Serve it hot with cauliflower in white sauce,
sauté potatoes and fried onions; or opt for jacket potatoes packed
with butter and a green salad.

1½lb (675g) pork sausage meat
6oz (175g) smooth and soft liver pâté
2 garlic cloves, peeled and crushed
2 tbsp Dubonnet (3 tbsp)
2 medium-sized eggs, beaten
2oz (50g) brown breadcrumbs (1 cup)
salt and pepper to taste

1 Mix sausage meat with liver pâté, garlic, Dubonnet, eggs and breadcrumbs. Season to taste with salt and pepper.
2 With damp hands, transfer mixture to baking tray (cookie sheet) lined with greased foil. Shape into an 8 x 5in (20 x 12·5cm) loaf.
3 Bake, uncovered, for 1 hour at 375°F (190°C), Gas 5. Remove from oven and serve cut into slices.

Fruited Liver with Brandy

(serves 4)

A mellow flavoured combination of liver and fruit which teams especially well
with Snow Potatoes (see page 43) and cooked green vegetables.

1oz (25g) butter (⅛ cup)
2oz (50g) onion, peeled and grated (about ½ cup)
1lb (450g) calves' or lambs' liver (16oz), diced
1 large dessert apple, peeled, cored and thinly sliced
1 level tsp salt (1½ level tsp)
1 tbsp brandy (1½ tbsp)
1 large banana

1 Heat butter in heavy frying pan or skillet. Add onion. Fry over low heat until dark gold.
2 Add liver, a few pieces at a time. Fry fairly briskly until well sealed and brown. Continue to fry more slowly, uncovered, for 7 minutes, turning.
3 Add apple and salt. Mix in well. Fry 5 minutes. Pour brandy into pan then slice in banana. Heat through 5 minutes, stirring once or twice.

Peppy Mexican Peppers

(serves 4)

A special for vegetarians are these mushroom and cheese-filled red peppers, simmered gently in vegetable stock and Mexican tequila. Serve with freshly cooked brown rice, and either fried or grilled tomato halves sprinkled with chopped fresh mint or parsley.

8 medium-sized red peppers, each 4oz or 100 to 125g (sweet red peppers)
1lb (450g) trimmed cap mushrooms (about 5 cups)
1 large onion, peeled
2 medium-sized eggs
2 rounded tbsp cornflour (3 rounded tbsp cornstarch)
1 level tsp salt (1 to 1¼ level tsp)
2oz (50g) grated Parmesan cheese (about ½ cup)
½pt (250ml) vegetable stock, reserved from cooking vegetables (1¼ cups)
2 tbsp tequila (3 tbsp)

1 Wash and dry peppers. Cut off tops and reserve for lids. Remove inside fibres and seeds. Stand upright in deepish pan, placing peppers close together so that they don't fall over.
2 To make filling, finely chop mushrooms and grate onion. Alternatively, chop in food processor. Transfer to bowl. Stir in eggs, cornflour (cornstarch), salt and cheese.
3 Mix thoroughly then spoon equal amounts into peppers. Top with pepper lids. Pour vegetable stock and tequila into pan. Slowly bring to boil.
4 Lower heat and cover. Simmer gently 40 to 45 minutes when peppers should be tender and filling lightly set. Serve hot with suggested accompaniments.

Fondue Neuchâtel

(*serves* 6)

Swiss fondue is one of the happier and more relaxed ways of entertaining, with quaint customs attached. For example, if a gentleman accidentally drops his bread into the melted cheese mixture, he must buy a bottle of wine for his fellow guests (or open another from his own collection). If a lady drops the bread, she has to kiss one of the men. If the same accident happens twice, the 'victim' has to throw another fondue party! Traditionally, fondue is a 'brew' of Swiss cheese, wine and kirsch, thickened with cornflour (cornstarch) and served with cubes of crusty French bread. It should be cooked in what the Swiss call a Caquelon; a wide and fairly shallow flameproof dish. The initial process takes place on top of the cooker, and then the dish is moved to a spirit stove on the table to keep hot. The recommended accompaniments are dry white wine or hot lemon tea—chilled beverages are incompatible.

1 large garlic clove
6oz (175g) Emmental cheese, grated (1½ cups)
1lb (450g) Gruyère cheese, grated (4 cups)
1 level tbsp cornflour (1¼ level tbsp cornstarch)
½pt (275ml) Swiss or Austrian dry white wine (1¼ cups)
1 tsp lemon juice (1½ tsp)
2 tbsp kirsch (3 tbsp)
white pepper to taste
1 long French loaf, cubed

1 Cut garlic in half. Press cut sides over base and sides of Caquelon or similar-sized flameproof dish (see above).
2 Add cheeses, cornflour, wine and lemon juice. Cook over low heat until cheese melts and mixture becomes fairly thick and creamy in consistency.
3 Stir in kirsch, season with pepper and stand dish on spirit stove.
4 To eat, spear cubes of bread onto forks and dip into cheese mixture. Swirl round, lift out and eat straight away.

Note Fondue tends to thicken on standing, but the addition of a large pinch of bicarbonate of soda thins it down again.

For Budget Fondue, use Cheddar cheese and cider. Omit kirsch.

For Beer Fondue, use Cheddar Cheese and beer. Omit kirsch.

For Dutch Cheese Dip, use Edam or Gouda, milk instead of wine, and gin instead of kirsch.

Desserts

Old English Trifle

More like the real thing, with egg-based custard sauce, sponge cake soaked in sherry, and a swirling crown of cream studded, as in Edwardian days, with multi-coloured hundreds and thousands.

1pt (575ml) warm milk

4 medium-sized eggs

2 egg yolks

2 level tbsp caster sugar (3 level tbsp granulated)

3 level tsp cornflour (4½ level tsp cornstarch)

6oz (175g) sponge cake

8 tbsp sweet sherry (12 tbsp)

3 rounded tbsp raspberry jam (4½ rounded tbsp raspberry preserve)

Topping

½pt (275ml) double cream (1¼ cups heavy cream)

2 rounded tbsp caster sugar (3 rounded tbsp granulated)

2 tbsp milk (3 tbsp)

2 rounded tsp hundreds and thousands (3 rounded tsp)

1 Beat milk thoroughly with whole eggs, egg yolks, sugar and cornflour (cornstarch).
2 Pour into heavy saucepan. Cook over low heat, whisking continuously, until custard thickens sufficiently to form a thin coating on the whisk. Bring just up to boil and remove from heat straight away. Leave aside temporarily.
3 Break up cake into large pieces and put into serving bowl. Soak with sherry. Top with blobs of jam. Add warm custard and gently stir with cake and other ingredients. Leave until completely cold.
4 Beat cream, sugar and milk together until thick. Swirl over trifle and refrigerate about 1 hour. Sprinkle with hundreds and thousands just before serving.

Zabaglione

(serves 4)

A masterpiece from the creative Italians, Zabaglione tastes like a mass of warm, delicate foam and may be served on its own with sponge fingers (boudoir biscuits or lady fingers) or as a topping for fruit (try fresh dates or oranges soaked in brandy). Traditionally it is made with egg yolks only and, when I was in Italy, I discovered that spirit is sometimes added as well.

4 egg yolks from large eggs
4 rounded tbsp caster sugar (6 rounded tbsp granulated)
4 tbsp marsala (6 tbsp)

1 Place yolks in basin over pan of gently simmering water. Add sugar.
2 Whisk until mixture is the texture of softly whipped cream, very light in texture and pale in colour. Gently whisk in marsala.
3 Spoon into 4 glasses and serve straight away.

Athol Brose

(serves 8)

A traditional oldie from Scotland, flavoured predictably with whisky.

4oz (125g) rolled oats (about 1 cup)
6 tbsp whisky (9 tbsp)
4 rounded tbsp clear honey, melted (6 rounded tbsp)
3tsp lemon juice ($4\frac{1}{2}$ tsp)
$\frac{1}{2}$pt (275ml) double cream ($2\frac{1}{2}$ cups heavy cream)

Decoration
2 level tbsp lightly toasted rolled oats (3 level tbsp)

1 Combine oats with whisky, melted honey and lemon juice. Cover. Leave to stand 2 hours for oats to soak up some of the liquid.
2 Whip cream until thick. Fold in oat mixture. Spoon into 8 glasses. Refrigerate 1 hour before serving. Sprinkle with toasted oats to decorate.

Advocaat and Banana Pancakes from Holland

(serves 8)

This combination marries two Dutch loves—pancakes and advocaat.

caster sugar (granulated)
8 freshly cooked pancakes minus Grand Marnier (see London Pancakes on page 124)
8 generous tbsp advocaat (12 tbsp)
4 medium-sized bananas

1 Sprinkle sugar over large sheet of greaseproof paper (wax paper) or foil. Stand a pancake on sugared surface.
2 Spread with 1 tbsp advocaat (1½ tbsp) then fill with half a sliced banana. Roll up. Repeat with rest of pancakes.
3 Transfer to a warm plate. Accompany with cream or ice cream.

Coffee Cream Meringue Cups

(serves 6)

I put this together for unexpected guests one Sunday lunchtime, grateful that I'd made and stored meringues some time in the past, and for my mini bottles of liqueur, the extra cream I'd ordered by chance from the milkman and my usual store of ice cream in the deep freeze. It's a devastatingly gluttonous sweet, but a special treat for happy occasions.

½pt (275ml) double cream (1¼ cups heavy cream)
3 tbsp Tia Maria or Kahlua (4½ tbsp)
8oz (225g) meringue
3 rounded tsp chocolate vermicelli (4½ rounded tsp)
about 1pt (575ml) vanilla ice cream (2½ cups)

1 Whip cream until softly stiff. Beat in coffee liqueur. Coarsely crumble meringue. Fold into cream mixture.
2 Scoop ice cream into 6 sundae glasses. Mound cream and meringue mixture on top. Sprinkle with chocolate vermicelli. Serve straight away.

Strawberry Mousse

(serves 8 to 10)

Elegant and classic, perfumed with ripe summer berries and Fraise liqueur.

1pt (575ml) strawberry purée (2½ cups), made from ripe, sweet berries
2 tbsp Fraise (3 tbsp)
¼pt (150ml) water (⅝ cup)
6 slightly rounded tsp (2 envelopes) powdered gelatine
(9 slightly rounded tsp unflavoured gelatin)
4 medium-sized eggs, separated
6oz (175g) caster sugar (about ¾ cup granulated)
½pt (275ml) double cream (1¼ cups heavy cream)

Decoration
3 kiwi fruit
12 whole strawberries

1 Combine strawberry purée with liqueur. Leave on one side temporarily.
2 Pour water into small saucepan. Shower in gelatine. Leave to stand 5 minutes. Heat very gently, without boiling, until gelatine completely dissolves. Cool.
3 Beat egg yolks with sugar until mixture is very thick, pale in colour and with the consistency of whipped cream.
4 Whisk in strawberry purée and melted gelatine. Leave in refrigerator until just beginning to thicken and set.
5 Beat egg whites to a stiff snow. Whip cream until thick. Fold alternatively into strawberry mixture and continue folding until absolutely smooth and all signs of streakiness have disappeared.
6 Pour into glass bowl. Refrigerate until set. Just before serving, peel kiwi fruit and thinly slice. Use to decorate top of mousse. Finally, add strawberries.

For Peach Mousse, use peach purée made from canned, drained fruit. Use apricot brandy, decorate with orange slices and raspberries.

Strawberry Sorbet

(serves 8)

Prettily pink and refreshingly cool, this sorbet is much less tricky to
make than people imagine.

8oz (225g) fresh strawberries (same)
2 tbsp Fraise (3 tbsp)
4oz (125g) caster sugar (½ cup granulated)
1 egg white

1 Wash and hull strawberries. Place into blender goblet or food processor with Fraise and
caster sugar.
2 Run machine until mixture forms a purée which is smooth and uniform in colour.
3 Pour into basin. Cover. Freeze 1½ hours. Whisk hard until fruit mixture is smooth and
all the ice crystals have been broken down.
4 Beat egg white to a stiff snow. Fold into sorbet. Return to basin. Cover. Freeze 4 to 5
hours or until firm.
5 To serve, leave to soften between 20 to 30 minutes at kitchen temperature. Scoop into
bowls and serve straight away.

For Raspberry Sorbet, use raspberries, 6oz (175g) sugar (¾ cup) and Framboise eau-de-vie.

For Kiwi Fruit Sorbet, use 4 large kiwi fruit, 4oz sugar and Cointreau.

Rumvocaat Figs

(serves 4)

For hurried moments, figs in Rumvocaat take seconds to prepare and, once
chilled and served with cream, make a superb and sophisticated dessert. For
dinner parties of 8 people, double the ingredients.

1 can (14oz or 397g) golden figs in syrup
3 tbsp Rumvocaat (4½ tbsp)

1 Tip figs and syrup from can into bowl. Stir in Rumvocaat. Cover. Chill.
2 Before serving, stir round and spoon into dishes. Coat with single cream (coffee cream).

Apricot Cream Crunch

(serves 6)

One of those sweets that looks as though it's taken hours to make, yet it can virtually be thrown together in under 15 minutes. It keeps well in the refrigerator, and can be confidently prepared at least 4 hours in advance.

1 can (15oz or 425g) apricot halves (2 cups)
1 tbsp Amaretto di Saronno (1½ tbsp)
½pt (275ml) double cream (1¼ cups heavy cream)
4 tbsp Siebrands cream liqueur (6 tbsp)
4 digestive biscuits (4 Graham crackers)
1 rounded tbsp flaked and toasted almonds (1½ rounded tbsp)

1 Mix apricots and syrup from can with the Amaretto di Saronna. Divide equally between 6 dishes.
2 Whip cream until thick. Stir in cream liqueur. Break biscuits into small pieces. Fold into cream mixture.
3 Spoon equal amounts over apricots then sprinkle with almonds.

Mexican Bananas

(serves 4)

One of the easiest sweets in the world, and a dream served with clouds of ice-cold whipped cream.

2oz (50g) butter (¼ cup)
4 medium-sized bananas
2 level tbsp soft brown sugar (3 level tbsp)
½ level tsp powdered cinnamon (¾ level tsp)
2 tbsp tequila (3 tbsp)

1 Heat butter until sizzling in frying pan. Add bananas. Fry 5 minutes, turning gently once or twice.
2 Sprinkle with sugar and cinnamon. Heat tequila separately in small pan until lukewarm. Flame.
3 Pour over bananas when flames have died down. Transfer contents of pan to 4 warm plates. Serve straight away.

Rice Cream Maltaise

(serves 8 to 10)

A rich yet refreshing sweet for special party occasions.

Rice Mixture
4oz (125g) American long grain rice (about $\frac{5}{8}$ cup)
$\frac{1}{2}$pt (275ml) cold water (1$\frac{1}{4}$ cups)
1pt (575ml) milk (2$\frac{1}{2}$ cups)

Gelatine Mixture
3 rounded tsp (1 envelope) gelatine (4$\frac{1}{2}$ rounded tsp unflavoured gelatin)
3 tbsp cold water (4$\frac{1}{2}$ tbsp)
4 medium-sized eggs, separated
4oz (125g) caster sugar ($\frac{1}{2}$ cup granulated)
$\frac{1}{4}$pt (150ml) milk ($\frac{5}{8}$ cup)
2 tbsp curaçao or Cointreau (3 tbsp)
$\frac{1}{2}$pt (275ml) double cream (1$\frac{1}{4}$ cups heavy cream)

Filling
4 medium-sized oranges, peeled and the flesh cut into segments
2 extra tbsp curaçao or Cointreau (3 tbsp)
1 level tsp grated orange peel (zest)
1 small sprig fresh mint

1 Put rice and water into large saucepan. Bring to boil. Stir round once. Cover. Lower heat. Cook over moderate heat for 15 minutes, when grains should be separate and fluffy and liquid absorbed.
2 Place cooked rice in top of double saucepan (boiler) or into basin standing over pan of gently simmering water. Stir in milk. Cook 40 minutes, uncovered, stirring from time to time.
3 Meanwhile, shower gelatine into cold water and leave to stand 5 minutes. Dissolve over very low heat but do not allow mixture to boil. Leave on one side to cool.
4 Beat egg yolks and sugar together until very thick and pale in colour. Stir in milk. Cook, stirring, over minimal heat until custard thickens sufficiently to coat back of spoon. Remove from heat. Stir in melted gelatine and orange liqueur.
5 Combine with rice mixture. Leave in the cool until just beginning to thicken and set. Beat egg whites to a stiff snow. Whip cream until thick.
6 Fold whites and cream alternately into rice mixture. When smooth and evenly combined, spread into a lightly oiled ring mould of 2pt (1·5 litre) capacity (5 cups).

7 Refrigerate until firm and set. Unmould onto serving dish. For filling, combine orange segments with orange liqueur and orange peel (zest). Spoon into centre of ring then add sprig of mint. If liked, decorate with orange slices.

Orange Pineapple Flambé

(serves 6)

Try this for special occasions and, if you can, flambé at the table—so much better for effect! It is the most gracious of sweets, and exquisitely refreshing.

2oz (50g) butter ($\frac{1}{4}$ cup)
6 thick slices of peeled pineapple
3 level tbsp dark, coarse cut marmalade ($4\frac{1}{2}$ level tbsp)
3 tbsp Galliano ($4\frac{1}{2}$ tbsp)
1 tbsp brandy ($1\frac{1}{2}$ tbsp)

1 Heat butter in large frying pan. Add pineapple. Fry 4 minutes, turning once. Stir in marmalade. Cook very slowly until melted.
2 Pour alcohol into small pan. Heat to lukewarm. Ignite.
3 Carefully trickle over pineapple in pan. Serve when flames have subsided. Accompany with ice cream.

No-time Cherry Brandy and Raspberry Mousse

(*serves 6*)

Pleasantly refreshing, this is the sort of sweet one keeps in reserve for
last-minute entertaining.

1 raspberry flavour jelly
¼pt (150ml) water (⅝ cup)
4 tbsp cherry brandy (6 tbsp)
extra water
1 carton (5oz or 142ml) soured cream (⅝ cup cultured soured cream), lightly chilled
2 egg whites
chopped walnuts or pecans

1 Place jelly in pan. Add water. Dissolve over minimal heat. Add cherry brandy.
2 Make up to ¾pt (425ml) (2 cups) with extra water. Leave in the cold until just beginning
to thicken and set. Whisk in soured cream.
3 Beat egg whites to a stiff snow. Fold into jelly mixture with a large metal spoon. Divide
equally between 6 dishes. Refrigerate until softly set before serving. Sprinkle with nuts.

A Special Kind of Syllabub

(*serves 6*)

Rapturously rich, eminently mellow and *not* for slimmers!

¾pt (425ml) double cream (2 cups heavy cream)
4 tbsp cold milk (6 tbsp)
3 heaped tbsp lemon curd (4½ heaped tbsp)
2 tbsp curaçao (3 tbsp)
1 tbsp dark rum (1½ tbsp)
1 packet (48 pieces) ratafias or 6 macaroons, broken into very small pieces

1 Beat cream and milk together until thick. Gently stir in lemon curd.
2 Add rest of ingredients and mix well with large metal spoon.
3 Transfer to wine-type glasses. Chill lightly before serving.

Harlequin Creams

(serves 6)

Cheeky, creamy and brightly tinted with red berries! Serve
frosty-cold from the fridge and accompany with
ice-cream wafers shaped like fans.

6oz (175g) fresh raspberries (about 1 cup)
2 tbsp Framboise (3 tbsp)
6 rounded tbsp granulated sugar (8 tbsp)
$\frac{1}{2}$pt (275ml) double cream ($1\frac{1}{4}$ cups heavy cream)
8oz (225g) strawberries (about $1\frac{1}{2}$ cups)
2 tbsp Fraise (3 tbsp)

1 Place raspberries in blender goblet with Framboise and half the sugar. Run machine until fruit forms a purée with other ingredients.
2 Whip cream until stiff. Gently fold in raspberry mixture. When smooth and evenly combined, divide equally between 6 wine-type glasses or sundae dishes.
3 Hull strawberries. Slice directly into blender goblet. Add rest of sugar and Fraise. Blend to a smooth purée.
4 Spoon evenly over cream mixture and you will find that the strawberries make their own way, forming a rippled or harlequin effect.
5 Refrigerate 2 to 3 hours before serving and add a wafer biscuit to each.

Mango Desserts

Any street market addict, shopping last thing on a Saturday, may be well pleased to find a touch of exotica going for the proverbial song. Such a stroke of good fortune happened to me, and the recipes which follow are the result of happy bargain hunting and a case of beautifully ripe mangoes.

Orange Mango and Amaretto à la Crème

(serves 6 to 8)

1 large, ripe mango (about 1lb or 450g)
4 rounded tbsp caster sugar (6 rounded tbsp granulated sugar)
8oz (about 250g) German Quark or French Fromage Blanc (low fat soft cheese made from skimmed milk)
finely grated peel of 1 medium-sized washed and dried orange (orange zest)
2 tbsp Amaretto di Saronno
$\frac{1}{4}$pt (150ml) double cream ($\frac{5}{8}$ cup heavy cream)
2 tbsp flaked almonds, lightly toasted (3 tbsp)

1 Peel mango and slice flesh directly into blender goblet or food processor. Add sugar. Run machine until fruit resembles a coarse purée.
2 Place cheese into bowl. Beat in mango purée, orange peel (zest) and Amaretto.
3 Whip cream until thick. Fold into mango mixture with large metal spoon. Transfer to 6 or 8 sundae glasses. Sprinkle each with almonds. Chill lightly before serving.

(*Top*) Unexpected Avocado Ice Cream, recipe on page 106 (*South African Avocados*)

(*Below*) Honey Rum Roulade with Walnuts, recipe on page 130 (*Gales Honey*)

Magical Mango Sorbet

(serves 6)

One of the simplest sorbets I know, and certainly one of the most refreshing.

1 large, ripe mango (about 1lb or 450g)
3 level tbsp caster sugar (4½ tbsp granulated sugar)
2 tbsp Bacardi (3 tbsp)
2 egg whites

1 Peel mango. Cut flesh directly into blender goblet or food processor. Add sugar and Bacardi.
2 Run machine until ingredients form a smooth purée. Transfer to bowl. Cover. Deep freeze until half set.
3 Beat mango mixture until smooth and free of ice crystals. Fold in egg whites, beaten to a stiff snow.
4 Return to bowl. Cover. Freeze until firm. Spoon or scoop into small bowls. Serve straight away.

South Pacific Fruit Bowl

(serves 8)

2 large, ripe mangoes (each about 1lb or 450g)
1 medium-sized ripe pineapple (about 3lb or 1½kg)
2 tbsp Cocoribe liqueur (3 tbsp)
2 kiwi fruit

1 Peel mangoes. Slice flesh directly into bowl so that no juice is lost. Peel pineapple, removing brown 'eyes' with top of potato peeler.
2 Cut pineapple into slices. Remove centre portion of hard core from each and discard. Cut flesh into small pieces. Mix with mangoes.
3 Add Cocoribe. Toss well. Transfer to glass serving bowl. Peel kiwis very thinly. Slice fruit. Arrange attractively on top of fruit salad. Cover. Chill lightly before serving. Accompany with coconut biscuits.

(Left) Apple and Rum Pie, recipe on page 110 *(French Wines)*

Orange and Coconut Layer Dessert

(serves 6 to 8)

A simple togetherness of readily available ingredients in a new form. Serve this memorable dessert well chilled with whipped cream or ice cream.

4 medium-sized oranges
3 large bananas
3 tbsp Drambuie (4½ tbsp)
3 level tbsp brown sugar (4½ tbsp)
1 level tsp cinnamon (1½ tsp)
3 heaped tbsp desiccated coconut (4½ tbsp)
2oz (50g) butter, melted (¼ cup)

1 Peel oranges, removing skin and pith. Slice oranges thinly. Use to cover base of about 10in (25cm) round, shallow heatproof dish.
2 Peel and slice bananas. Arrange over oranges in single layer. Add Drambuie.
3 Sprinkle with sugar and cinnamon. Top with a layer of coconut. Trickle melted butter over the top.
4 Brown lightly under a hot grill for 2 minutes. Cool. Chill about 1 to 2 hours in the refrigerator before serving with a bowl of whipped cream.

Coffee Whisky Liqueur Ice Cream

(serves 10 to 12)

A velvety-smooth ice cream which is a joy with the Marshmallow Fudge Sauce given below.

1 level tbsp instant coffee powder or granules (1½ tbsp)
2 tbsp boiling water (3 tbsp)
½pt (275ml) double cream ⎫
¼pt (150ml) single cream ⎭ (2 cups heavy cream)
2 egg yolks
4 rounded tbsp caster sugar (6 rounded tbsp)
7 tbsp coffee whisky liqueur (about 10 tbsp)
2 egg whites

1 Dissolve instant coffee in the water. Leave to cool completely. Whip creams together until thick. Stir in egg yolks, sugar, coffee whisky liqueur and cooled coffee.
2 Beat egg whites to a stiff snow. Fold into coffee cream mixture. Transfer to basin. Cover securely. Freeze until half frozen.
3 Beat until smooth. Cover again. Freeze until hard. To serve, leave ice cream to soften a little at room temperature. Scoop into dishes. Either eat as it is or coat with Marshmallow Fudge Sauce.

Marshmallow Fudge Sauce

(Enough for half the ice cream)

4oz (125g) butter ($\frac{1}{2}$ cup)
3oz (75g) soft brown sugar ($\frac{3}{8}$ cup)
4oz (125g) marshmallows (same)
2 tbsp double cream (3 tbsp heavy cream)
2 tsp whisky (3 tsp)

1 Put first four ingredients into heavy pan. Melt slowly over low heat, stirring continuously.
2 Bring to boil, still stirring. Boil gently 3 minutes. Remove from heat. Stir in whisky. Use as required.

Pineapple Cool Sticks

(serves 6)

When a neighbour of mine was scratching the barrel looking for starters, I came up with two ideas—grapefruit with crème de menthe and then pineapple. Both, as it happened, proved to be winners but we preferred the grapefruit for starters and this pineapple version as the perfect sweet to end a buxom meal.

1 medium-sized pineapple (about 2lb or 900g)
3 tbsp crème de menthe ($4\frac{1}{2}$ tbsp)
fresh mint sprigs

1 Peel pineapple, removing 'eyes' with a potato peeler. Cut lengthwise into strips, removing central core.
2 Cut strips into halves or thirds, depending on size, and transfer to shallow dish.
3 Sprinkle with crème de menthe. Cover. Refrigerate 3 to 4 hours. Before serving, arrange sticks on 6 individual plates. Decorate with mint sprigs.

Pineapple in a Dream

(serves 8)

Another of those non-complicated sweets to impress your guests. A mix of six ingredients gives you eight stunning sundaes with a taste of the tropics.

1 large pineapple (about 3lb or 1½kg)
1½ tbsp each Mandarin Napoléan and crème de bananes liqueurs (2¼ tbsp each)
¼pt (150ml) double cream (⅝ cup heavy cream), chilled but not frozen
2 tbsp Fraise liqueur (3 tbsp)
1 heaped tbsp desiccated coconut, toasted (1½ tbsp)
4 glacé cherries, halved

1 Peel pineapple, removing 'eyes' with a potato peeler. Cut into slices, removing central core. Cut up flesh and put into bowl. Stir in liqueur.
2 Divide between 8 sundae glasses. Chill at least 2 hours in the refrigerator.
3 Before serving, whip cream with the Fraise liqueur until thick. Swirl equal amounts over pineapple in glasses, sprinkle with coconut and top each with half a cherry.

Unexpected Avocado Ice Cream

(serves 10 to 12)

A tantalising and unusual ice cream, adapted from a South African recipe.

1 fully ripe, large avocado
2 tsp lemon juice (3 tsp)
1 tbsp clear honey (1½ tbsp)
2 tbsp Cointreau (3 tbsp)
2 egg whites (from large eggs)
1pt (575ml) double cream (2½ cups heavy cream)
4 rounded tbsp caster sugar (6 rounded tbsp granulated sugar)

Decoration
1oz (25g) shelled pecan nuts (¼ cup)
1 fully ripe, small avocado
extra lemon juice

106

1 Peel large avocado as you would peel a pear, starting at the pointed end.
2 Cut flesh directly into blender goblet or food processor. Add lemon juice, honey and Cointreau. Blend to a smooth and fine purée. Pour into large bowl.
3 In clean and dry bowl, beat egg whites to stiff snow. In separate bowl, whip cream until thick. Fold in sugar.
4 Fold egg whites and two-thirds of the cream alternately into avocado purée mixture. When smooth and evenly combined, transfer to a straight-sided round dish (a soufflé dish for example) large enough to take the ice cream with a 2inch (5cm) gap at the top.
5 Cover with cling film, and deep freeze until firm and set; about 6 to 8 hours. To serve, dip bowl briefly in hot water to loosen ice cream.
6 Invert onto a serving dish and decorate with remaining cream, pecan nuts and slices of peeled avocado, first brushed with lemon juice to stop browning. Serve straight away with wafers.

Note Do not leave the ice cream in hot water for more than a few seconds as it will melt; plunge the bowl in and out of the water four or five times, which should take about 10 seconds. If the ice cream refuses to shift, give it another 10 seconds.
If preferred, spoon or scoop ice cream on to dishes and decorate with cream, nuts and slices of avocado as described above.

Perfume of Summer Fruit Salad

(*serves 8*)

Enchantingly coloured, with the bouquet and fragrance of an old-fashioned summer garden.

4 large, ripe peaches, blanched and skinned
fresh lemon juice
2lb (900g) strawberries
6 tbsp apricot brandy (9 tbsp)
3 heaped tbsp icing sugar, sifted (4½ heaped tbsp sifted confectioner's sugar)
2 level tbsp pine kernels (available from health food shops and speciality food shops)
(3 level tbsp)

1 Halve peaches and remove stones. Cut fruit into slices. Sprinkle with lemon juice. Transfer to large bowl.
2 Wash and hull strawberries. Slice. Add to bowl with apricot brandy and icing sugar. Stir well to mix.
3 Cover. Chill at least 4 hours in the refrigerator for flavours to combine. Sprinkle with pine kernels before serving. Accompany with single cream (coffee cream).

Palm Tree Fruit Compôte

(serves 8)

Unusual and fragrant, this is a colourful fruit combination for autumn and winter.

1 medium, ripe pineapple

4 tbsp crème de bananes (6 tbsp)

1 medium-sized, ripe melon

2 large oranges, peeled

2 medium-sized, red-skinned dessert apples, washed and dried but left unpeeled

1 medium-sized, ripe avocado

1 kiwi fruit

1 Peel pineapple, removing 'eyes' with potato peeler. Slice and remove core. Cut remaining pineapple rings into small pieces. Transfer to glass bowl. Add crème de bananes. Stir well to mix.

2 Halve melon, discarding seeds. Scoop flesh into bowl with melon baller or spoon. Peel oranges, removing all traces of white pith. Slice, then cut into segments. Add to bowl.

3 Quarter apples and core. Cut quarters into dice. Peel avocado as you would peel a pear, starting from the pointed end. Dice flesh. Peel kiwi fruit. Thinly slice. Add all three fruits to bowl.

4 Stir well. Cover. Refrigerate overnight before serving to give flavours a chance to mix and mature.

Fruit Salad Noel

(serves 6 to 8)

Designed especially for Christmas, this warm-hearted fruit salad is packed with spice, laced with wine and spiked with pecans. Serve it with thick, flowing cream and small, sweet biscuits coated with dark, velvety chocolate.

8oz (225g) *each* black and green grapes, halved and seeded

4oz (125g) fresh dates, coarsely chopped

2 medium-sized oranges, peeled and divided into segments

2 dessert apples, peeled, cored and sliced

2 large bananas, peeled and sliced

108

$\frac{1}{4}$pt (150ml) rosé wine ($\frac{5}{8}$ cup)

$\frac{1}{4}$pt (150ml) water

3 tbsp honey, melted (4$\frac{1}{2}$ tbsp)

1 tbsp lemon juice (1$\frac{1}{2}$ tbsp)

2 cloves

2oz (50g) pecan nuts ($\frac{1}{2}$ cup)

1 Place all prepared fruit into large bowl.
2 Pour wine and water into pan. Add honey, lemon juice and cloves. Heat until hot, but do not boil. Remove cloves.
3 Pour over fruit and leave to cool. Stir in pecans. Cover. Refrigerate about 2 hours before serving .

Firebird Fruit 'Stew'

(*serves 8*)

A hot fruit salad makes an interesting talking point, especially when it's laced with cherry brandy and served with vanilla ice cream.

$\frac{1}{4}$pt (150ml) water ($\frac{5}{8}$ cup)

8oz (225g) caster sugar (1 cup granulated sugar)

8oz (225g) rhubarb, trimmed and chopped (2 cups)

12oz (350g) sliced strawberries (about 3 cups)

12oz (350g) black cherries, stoned (about 2 cups)

4oz (125g) raspberries ($\frac{2}{3}$ cup)

1$\frac{1}{2}$lb (675g) red watermelon, de-seeded and diced

3 tbsp cherry brandy (4$\frac{1}{2}$ tbsp)

1 Heat water until hot in large saucepan. Add sugar. Stir until dissolved over low heat. Add rhubarb. Simmer until just tender but do not overcook, or fruit might fall to pieces.
2 Add all remaining fruits with cherry brandy. Heat through until hot. Serve with scoops of ice cream.

Apple and Rum Pie

(*serves 8*)

A splendid pie made with Golden Delicious apples and rum.
Serve with mellow Sauternes, and nibbles of
Cheddar cheese, toasted almonds, exotic kumquats and sultanas (golden raisins).
The pastry should be made with 8oz (225g) flour (2 cups) and 4oz (125g) butter or
margarine, etc.

shortcrust pastry
6 Golden Delicious apples
6oz (175g) caster sugar ($\frac{3}{4}$ cup granulated)
1 level tsp cinnamon
1oz (25g) butter, melted ($\frac{1}{8}$ cup)
2 tbsp dark rum

Glaze
1 egg yolk from small egg
2 tbsp single cream (3 tbsp coffee cream)

1 Divide pastry into 2 pieces, making one slightly larger than the other. Use the smaller piece to line an 8in (20cm) well buttered pie plate (pie pan) with rim.
2 Peel, quarter and core apples. Cut into thin slices, directly into large bowl. Add all remaining ingredients. Toss over and over until well mixed. Pile into pie plate, doming up filling in centre.
3 Moisten edges of pastry with water. Cover with lid, rolled and cut from rest of pastry. Press edges well together to seal. Brush with glaze, made by beating egg yolk and cream well together. Make a few slits in top to allow steam to escape.
4 If liked, decorate with pastry cut-outs and brush with more glaze. Place in oven pre-heated to 450°F (230°C), Gas 8. Bake 10 minutes.
5 Reduce heat to 350°F (180°C), Gas 4. Continue to bake a further 35 to 45 minutes or until apples are tender.
6 Remove from oven, cut into wedges and serve hot with a jug of single cream (coffee cream). If preferred, accompany with whipped cream or vanilla ice cream.

Omelet Soufflé Surprise

(*serves 6*)

Also called Baked Alaska or Norwegian Omelet, hotels regard this as the 'pièce de résistance' of any meal, and in Bulgaria vast dishes of the soufflé are brought impressively to the table, aflame with plum brandy. My version is less dramatic!

1 x 7in (17·5cm) round of plain cake, about 1in (2·5cm) thick
4 tbsp sweet sherry (6 tbsp)
1 1¾pt (1 litre) round tub of vanilla ice cream (just over 4¼ cups)
3 egg whites from large eggs
squeeze of lemon juice
6oz (175g) caster sugar (¾ cup granulated)
6 glacé cherries, halved
1 piece stem ginger in syrup, drained and sliced
12 diamonds cut from angelica

1 Stand cake in large, heatproof dish which is shallow rather than deep.
2 Moisten with sherry. Stand block of ice cream on top. Leave in deep freeze temporarily.
3 Whisk egg whites and lemon juice together to form a stiff snow. Gradually whisk in one-third of the sugar.
4 Continue to whisk until very stiff. Beat in next third of sugar. Finally stir in remaining sugar.
5 Remove cake and ice cream from deep freeze. Cover *completely* with egg white meringue. Decorate with cherries, ginger and angelica.
6 'Flash' bake about 3 minutes in oven set to 450°F (230°C). Gas 8, when meringue should be lightly flecked with gold.
7 Remove from oven, cut into wedges and serve straight away.

'Nursery' Pear Pudding

(serves 6)

Not for little children with its blanket of cassis, but for
grown men who unfailingly drool over sweet and gooey puddings.
This is just such a pudding, geared
for your nearest and dearest, and gluts of garden pears. It's
an easy-mix affair with minimal effort involved.

8oz (225g) self-raising flour (2 cups all-purpose with $4\frac{1}{2}$ level tsp double-acting
baking powder)
1 level tsp baking powder ($1\frac{1}{2}$ extra level tsp double-acting baking powder)
6oz (175g) soft margarine ($\frac{3}{4}$ cup)
6oz (175g) caster sugar ($\frac{3}{4}$ cup granulated)
2 large eggs (room temperature)
3 ripe dessert pears
3 tbsp cassis ($4\frac{1}{2}$ tbsp)

1 Well grease a 2pt ($1\frac{1}{4}$ litre) ovenproof dish. Set oven to 375°F (190°C), Gas 5.
2 Place flour, baking powder, margarine, sugar and eggs into mixing bowl. Beat steadily
for 3 minutes or until well blended and smooth.
3 Peel and core pears. Dice. Stir into pudding mixture. Spread into prepared dish. Bake
1 hour or until well risen and golden.
4 Turn out onto warm serving dish and coat with cassis. Cut into wedges and serve
straight away with cream.

Plum Pudding

(makes 2 puddings, each enough for 10 servings)

No book containing desserts in any shape or form would be complete without
Plum or Christmas Pudding, so here is an old faithful, with Brandy Butter.

4oz (125g) plain flour (1 cup all-purpose)
1 level tsp mixed spice ($1\frac{1}{2}$ level tsp)
8oz (225g) fresh white breadcrumbs (4 cups)
8oz (225g) soft brown sugar (1 cup)

112

10oz (275g) finely shredded suet (about 1½ cups)
1½lb (675g) mixed dried fruit (about 4¼ to 4½ cups)
2oz (50g) mixed chopped peel (about ½ cup loosely packed)
4oz (125g) cooking dates, chopped (about 1 cup loosely packed)
4 heaped tbsp chopped walnuts or toasted almonds (6 heaped tbsp)
1 tbsp maraschino (1½ tbsp) (optional)
4 large eggs
1 tsp vanilla essence (1½ tsp vanilla extract)
1 level tsp finely grated tangerine peel (1½ level tsp)
4 tbsp brandy, whisky or rum (6 tbsp)
1 tbsp black treacle (1½ tbsp molasses)
¼pt (150ml) dark beer for mixing (⅝ cup)

1 Sift flour and spice into very large bowl. Add crumbs, sugar, suet, mixed dried fruit, chopped peel, dates and nuts.
2 Stir in all remaining ingredients. Mix thoroughly. Leave to stand, covered, overnight. To cook, divide between two 3pt (1·75 litre) basins (7½ cups) which should be heavily greased.
3 Cover with double thickness of greased, greaseproof (wax) paper then overwrap with foil. Place in 2 pans. Half fill each with boiling water.
4 Cook steadily for 6 hours, topping up pans with water occasionally to prevent drying out. Leave puddings to cool to lukewarm then turn out of basins.
5 When completely cold, wrap in greaseproof paper then overwrap again in foil. Store in a cool and airy cupboard or, if room, in the refrigerator. Resteam each pudding for 2 to 3 hours before serving.

Brandy Butter

(serves 10)

Known also as Brandy Hard Sauce, this is a delectable confection to serve with Christmas Pudding.

Cream 8oz (225g) softened butter (1 cup) with 8oz (225g) caster sugar (1 cup granulated). When very light and fluffy, beat in 4 tbsp brandy (6 tbsp) and, if liked, mixed spice to taste. Spoon into a small serving bowl and chill until hard.

Rum Butter

(serves 10)

Make as Brandy Butter but use rum instead of brandy.

Crèpes Annette

(*serves 4*)

Why should Suzette have all the fame and acclaim when so many other bright young things from the twenties and thirties had such deliciously nostalgic names? As a tribute to all that was, here are nine variations on the Suzette theme using a mixed bag of spirits to stop yours flagging!

8 freshly cooked pancakes (made as given in Seafood Galettes, page 20)
4oz (125g) butter (½ cup)
1 rounded tbsp caster sugar (1½ rounded tbsp)
4 tbsp Kahlua or Tia Maria (6 tbsp)
2 tbsp brandy (3 tbsp)

1 Fold pancakes in half and then in half again. Melt butter in large pan over low heat.
2 Add sugar and Kahlua or Tia Maria. Heat until sugar melts. Add folded pancakes. Swish about in the pan liquor, turning once.
3 Heat through 5 minutes. Meanwhile, heat brandy to lukewarm in small pan. Ignite. Pour over pancakes. Serve when flames have subsided.

For Crèpes Babette, substitute 4 tbsp Parfait Amour (6 tbsp), a violet-coloured and flavoured liqueur, for the Kahlua or Tia Maria. Use French Mirabelle eau-de-vie in place of the brandy for flaming. (Or try any of the other plum liqueurs from the Balkans, such as slivovitz).

For Crèpes Claudette, substitute 4 tbsp (6 tbsp) crème de cacao for the Kahlua or Tia Maria. Use navy rum in place of the brandy for flaming.

For Crèpes Georgette, substitute 4 tbsp green or yellow Chartreuse (6 tbsp) for the Kahlua or Tia Maria. Use vodka in place of the brandy for flaming.

For Crèpes Ginette, substitute 4 tbsp cherry brandy (6 tbsp) for the Kahlua or Tia Maria. Use gin in place of the brandy for flaming.

For Crèpes Ninette, substitute 5 tbsp crème de bananes (7½ tbsp) for the Kahlua or Tia Maria. Use whisky in place of the brandy for flaming.

For Crèpes Paulette, substitute 4 tbsp mandarin liqueur (6 tbsp) for the Kahlua or Tia Maria and add 1 level tsp finely grated lemon peel (1½ level tsp) to the pancakes as they are heating. Use Armagnac in place of the brandy for flaming.

For Crêpes Suzette, substitute 4 tbsp Grand Marnier, Cointreau or curaçao (6 tbsp) for the Kahlua or Tia Maria, and add 1 level tsp *each* of finely grated orange and lemon peel (1½ level tsp) to the pancakes as they are heating. Use brandy for flaming.

For Crêpes Yvette, substitute 6 tbsp advocaat (9 tbsp) for the Kahlua or Tia Maria, and add the juice of 2 medium-sized oranges while the pancakes are heating. Use maraschino or kirsch in place of the brandy for flaming.

Strawberry Almond Pudding

(serves 6 to 8)

One of those cosy, soft-textured and airy puddings that always appeals.

6oz (175g) caster sugar (¾ cup granulated)
6oz (175g) butter or block margarine, at kitchen temperature (¾ cup)
3 medium-sized eggs
2oz (50g) ground almonds (about ¼ cup)
8oz (225g) hulled strawberries, washed and sliced (about 1½ cups)
8oz (225g) self-raising flour, sifted (2 cups all-purpose with 2 level tsp double-acting baking powder)
3 tbsp milk (4½ tbsp)
4 tbsp Amaretto di Saronno (6 tbsp)
custard sauce or single cream (coffee cream) for serving

1 Well butter a 3pt (1·75 litre) dish (7½ cups). Set oven to 350°F (180°C), Gas 4.
2 Tip sugar into a bowl. Add butter or margarine. Cream thoroughly until very light and fluffy. Beat in eggs, one at a time, adding 2 tsp ground almonds (3 tsp) with each.
3 Stir in rest of almonds and strawberries. Gradually fold in flour alternately with milk.
4 When smooth and well mixed, spread evenly into prepared dish. Bake 1¼ hours or until pudding is well risen and golden brown.
5 Turn out of dish and moisten with the Amaretto. Serve straight away.

French Gooseberry Clafouti

(*serves 8*)

Reminiscent of Britain's baked batter pudding with fruit, the French version is more like a baked egg custard and is a comforting dessert for cool days.

2 cans (each 10oz or 284g) gooseberries
3 level tbsp plain flour (4½ level tbsp all-purpose)
pinch of salt
5 level tbsp caster sugar (7½ tbsp granulated)
3 large eggs
¾pt (425ml) milk (2 cups)
2 tbsp peach or apricot brandy or French Mirabelle (3 tbsp)

1 Drain gooseberries, reserving syrup. Spread fruit over base of 2pt (1¼ litre) shallow ovenproof dish (5 cups), which should be thickly buttered.
2 Sift flour and salt into bowl. Add 3 tbsp sugar (4½ tbsp). Beat in whole eggs, then whisk in milk. Continue to whisk until bubbly then pour over gooseberries.
3 Bake 30 to 40 minutes in hot oven set to 425°F (220°C), Gas 7, when Clafouti should be golden brown. Remove from oven. Sprinkle with rest of sugar. Serve with reserved syrup heated until hot with the spirit.

Ginger Cheese Cake with Cointreau

(*serves 10*)

Easily assembled and always popular with everyone, the cheese cakes which follow have all been tastefully enhanced with fruit or spices and alcohol, and are useful as a dessert both for informal and formal occasions. Cheese cakes keep several days in the refrigerator, but do not take kindly to deep freezing.

4oz (125g) digestive biscuits, crushed (about ½ cup Graham crackers, crushed)
4oz (125g) stem ginger, drained and thinly sliced (same)
1½lb (675g) curd cheese (about 3 cups)
4oz (125g) unsalted butter, melted (½ cup)
6oz (175g) caster sugar (⅔ cup granulated)
3 medium-sized eggs, kitchen temperature
2 level tbsp cornflour (3 level tbsp cornstarch)

2 tbsp Cointreau (3 tbsp)
1 tsp vanilla essence (1½ tsp vanilla extract)
1 level tsp finely grated lemon peel (1½ level tsp)

1 For a deep cake, brush an 8in (20cm) spring-clip tin (spring pan form) with melted butter. For a shallower cake treat a 10in (25cm) tin (pan) in the same way. Set oven to 300°F (150°C), Gas 2.
2 Cover base of tin evenly with crushed biscuits then top with sliced ginger.
3 Place cheese in basin. Beat in butter, sugar, whole eggs, cornflour (cornstarch), Cointreau, vanilla and lemon peel.
4 When smooth and evenly combined, pour into tin over biscuits and ginger. Tap tin gently to remove air bubbles. Bake about 1½ hours for the deep cake; 1 hour for the shallow one.
5 Switch off oven and leave cake to finish cooking in the residual heat. If the cake starts browning, remove from oven straight away.
6 When completely cold, unclip sides and remove. Leave cake on its metal base and place on serving dish before cutting and serving.

Note The texture and flavour are greatly improved if the cake is refrigerated 2 to 3 hours before cutting and serving.

For Mandarin Cheese Cake with Bénédictine, cover biscuits with 1 drained can mandarins instead of ginger. Flavour cheese mixture with 2 tbsp Bénédictine (3 tbsp) instead of Cointreau.

For Cherry Cheese Cake with Maraschino, cover biscuits with 1 small can (about 7½oz or 213g) drained and stoned red cherries (1 cup) instead of ginger. Flavour cheese mixture with 2 tbsp maraschino liqueur (3 tbsp) and about ½ tsp almond essence (extract) instead of Cointreau.

For Peach Cheese Cake with Amaretto, cover biscuits with 1 can (about 14½oz or 411g) drained peach slices (about 2 cups) instead of ginger. Flavour cheese mixture with 2 tbsp Amaretto di Saronno (3 tbsp), instead of Cointreau.

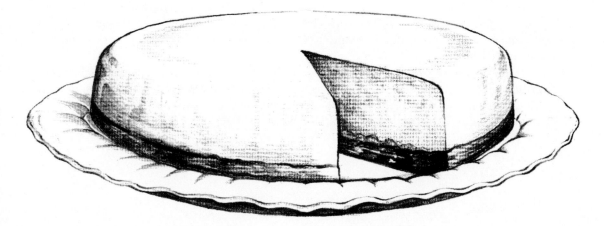

Kissing Cake

(serves 10 to 12)

When it's kisses all round at some important celebration, what better
dessert than this sumptuous, cream and berry laden, rich dessert
cake with its feather-light texture and elegant, sophisticated appearance?

5 large eggs, kitchen temperature

5oz (150g) caster sugar ($\frac{5}{8}$ cup granulated)

4oz (100g) plain flour (1 cup all-purpose)

1oz (25g) cornflour ($\frac{1}{4}$ cup cornstarch)

1 level tsp baking powder ($1\frac{1}{4}$ level tsp)

3 tbsp sweet sherry

$\frac{3}{4}$pt (425ml) double cream ($1\frac{1}{2}$ cups heavy cream)

3 tbsp cold milk

1lb (450g) small strawberries or raspberries (16oz) (or berry jam)

1 Brush a 10in (25cm) spring pan form (a cake tin with clip-on sides, usually recommended for cheese cake) with melted butter. Line base and sides with greaseproof paper.
Brush with more butter. Alternatively, line base and sides with non-stick parchment
paper.

2 Break eggs, one at a time, into large basin standing over a pan of hot water. Whisk
until foamy. Gradually add sugar. Continue to whisk until mixture becomes as thick as
softly whipped cream, about three times its original volume and very pale in colour.

3 Sift flour, cornflour (cornstarch) and baking powder directly on to a plate. Return to
sieve. Shake over whisked eggs and sugar.

4 Using a large metal spoon, fold dry ingredients gently into egg and sugar mixture,
taking care not to beat.

5 Transfer to prepared tin. Bake 45 minutes in oven set to 350°F (180°C), Gas 4. Remove
from oven. Leave 15 minutes in which time cake will fall slightly and top will wrinkle.
Unclip sides.

6 When cake is completely cold, invert on to a piece of greaseproof paper dusted with
sifted icing sugar. Carefully cut into 3 layers horizontally. Sprinkle each layer with
sherry.

7 Whip cream and milk together until thick. Reserve 12 of the best strawberries for
decoration, and halve. Slice remainder. Or reserve 24 of the best raspberries, leaving
remainder whole.

8 Sandwich layers together with cream and sliced strawberries or whole raspberries.
Spread more cream over top. Transfer to plate. Using a star-shaped tube and icing bag,
pipe lines of cream round sides of cake then decorate top with more cream as shown in
picture opposite. Add berries. Chill lightly before serving.

Gulab Jamun

Many Eastern desserts are characterised by their sweetness and fragrance. India's Gulab Jamun is no exception and for those who have enjoyed the little syrup-soaked, fried dumplings in Indian restaurants, here is an adaptation of the traditional recipe with apricot brandy added. This fruity liqueur plays magical tricks with the flavour of the syrup, and rounds the whole thing off to perfection. Gulab Jamum may be served warm.

3oz (75g) full cream milk powder (6 to 7 rounded tbsp)

1½oz (40g) plain flour (4 level tbsp all-purpose)

½ level tsp baking powder (¾ level tsp double-acting baking powder)

1oz (25g) unsalted butter (⅛ cup)

4 tbsp cold water to mix (5 to 6 tbsp)

corn oil for frying

Syrup

6oz (175g) caster sugar (¾ cup granulated sugar)

¼pt (150ml) water (⅝ cup)

4 whole cardamoms, tapped lightly until they crack open

2 tbsp triple rose water (3 tbsp) or few drops rose essence (extract)

1 tbsp apricot brandy (1½ tbsp)

6 saffron strands (optional)

1 Sift milk powder, flour and baking powder into bowl. Rub in butter finely. (As though making pastry).

2 Using a fork, mix to a firmish dough with the water. Shape into 12 even-sized balls.

3 Half fill a medium-sized saucepan with oil. Heat until hot, but not as hot as for chips for example.

4 Add the balls, 3 or 4 at a time. Fry between 4 and 5 minutes when they should be a warm gold all over and almost double their original size.

5 Lift out of pan. Drain on crumpled kitchen paper and leave on one side temporarily while preparing syrup.

6 Tip sugar into pan. Add water. Dissolve slowly over low heat. Add cardamoms. Remove from heat. Stir in rose water, apricot brandy and saffron (if used). Pour into dish.

7 Add fried Gulab Jamun and gently toss round and round in the syrup. Leave to soak until cold. Spoon into small dishes, allowing 2 per person, with some syrup.

Simnel Cake, recipe on page 122 (*French Wines*)

Simnel Cake

(serves 15)

The best dessert imaginable for Mothering Sunday, and an exquisitely flavoured cake with a festive traditional air. To cut down on cooking time, I have adopted an American technique and used a spring pan form which consists of a base and clip-on sides; the sort of tin most commonly used for cheesecake. Although the cake is traditionally British, both the recipe and photograph (page 120) are from the USA.

5oz (150g) sultanas (1 cup seedless white raisins)

5oz (150g) currants (1 cup)

6oz (175g) glacé cherries, halved (1 cup candied cherries)

3oz (75g) mixed chopped peel ($\frac{1}{2}$ cup mixed candied peel, chopped)

4 fl oz (125ml) brandy ($\frac{1}{2}$ cup)

8oz (225g) unsalted Dutch butter (1 cup sweet butter)

peel of 2 washed lemons, grated (minced)

8oz (225g) caster sugar (1 cup granulated)

4 medium-sized eggs, room temperature

9oz (250g) plain flour, sifted ($2\frac{1}{2}$ cups cake flour)

$1\frac{1}{2}$lb (675g) ready-made almond paste

little extra beaten egg

5oz (150g) icing sugar, sifted (1 cup confectioner's sugar)

warm water

$\frac{1}{2}$ tsp vanilla essence

Decorations

assorted food colourings

thin strips of angelica or crystallised lime peel (candied angelica or candied lime peel)

ribbon

1 Place sultanas (white raisins), currants, cherries and mixed peel into bowl. Stir in brandy. Cover. Leave to stand overnight.

2 Line base and sides of 8in (20cm) spring pan form with greased greaseproof paper or non-stick parchment paper. Set oven to 300°F (160°C), Gas 3.

3 Cream butter with lemon peel and sugar until light and fluffy. Beat in whole eggs, one at a time, adding a heaped tbsp ($1\frac{1}{2}$ tbsp) flour with each.

4 Fold in brandy-soaked fruits alternately with rest of flour. Spread half into prepared tin. Roll out one-third almond paste into 7in (17·5cm) round. Place on top of cake mixture to form middle layer.

122

5 Spread evenly with rest of cake mixture. Bake 1¼ to 1½ hours, when cake should be risen and golden brown. To test, push a wooden cocktail stick (pick) in the centre. If it comes out clean, the cake is done.

6 Remove from oven. Leave to stand 10 minutes before unclipping sides of tin and lifting off. Transfer cake to baking tray (cookie sheet).

7 To decorate, roll half of the remaining almond paste into 15 small balls and stand in a border round top of cake, about 1in (2·5cm) in from edge. Secure to cake with melted jam.

8 Brush balls with beaten egg and bake until lightly browned, allowing about 8 minutes in oven set to 375°F (180°C), Gas 5.

9 When completely cold, make a fairly thick glacé icing (glaze) with sugar, a few tsp water and vanilla. Spoon onto centre of cake, spreading it over top to meet the balls. The best implement to use is the back of a teaspoon.

10 Mould rest of almond paste into different fruits, colouring them with appropriate food colourings. Allow about 6 hours to dry, then place on cake as shown in the picture.

11 Add strips of angelica or lime peel to represent grass, and finally tie ribbon round the sides. Serve in small portions, as it is very rich.

London Pancakes

(*serves 8*)

To add a touch of 'oranges and lemons' to the London Pancakes, I have included
Grand Marnier in the batter mixture and, traditionally, served them
sprinkled with lemon juice and rolled in sugar.

Batter Mixture
4oz (125g) plain flour (1 cup all-purpose)
pinch of salt
2 medium-sized eggs
1oz (25g) butter, melted ($\frac{1}{8}$ cup)
$\frac{1}{4}$pt (150ml) cold water ($\frac{5}{8}$ cup)
$\frac{1}{4}$pt (150ml) cold milk ($\frac{5}{8}$ cup)
2 tbsp Grand Marnier (3 tbsp)
melted white cooking fat for frying (melted shortening)
fresh lemon juice for sprinkling
caster sugar for rolling (granulated)
halved lemon slices for decoration

1 To make batter, sift flour and salt into basin. Add eggs and butter. Gradually whisk in water. When batter is smooth and well blended, beat briskly for a good 5 minutes.
2 Gently stir in milk and Grand Marnier. Cover. Refrigerate 1 hour. To make pancakes, brush a fairly large and heavy frying pan with a thin application of melted fat (shortening).
3 Heat until hot. Pour in sufficient batter to form a *thin* pancake over base, tilting pan in all directions to make sure mixture flows to edges. Fry until golden. Turn over. Fry other side until brown and speckly.
4 To keep hot, turn out onto a large plate over a pan of gently boiling water. Cook rest of batter in the same way, making a total of 8 pancakes stacked on top of each other over the water.
5 Take each pancake individually and stand on a piece of foil or greaseproof paper coated with sugar. Sprinkle with lemon juice and roll up.
6 Transfer to a warm dish and decorate with lemon slices. Serve straight away.

Black Forest Sundaes

(serves 4)

Anything, it seems, on the Black Forest/chocolate/cherry/kirsch theme seems to climb straight to the top of the culinary hit parade, so here are a few desserts to set you on your way, with the famous Black Forest Cherry Gateau included.

1 can (about 8oz or 225g) black cherries (about 1 cup)
2 tbsp kirsch (3 tbsp)
chocolate ice cream
4 heaped tbsp whipped cream (6 heaped tbsp)
4 glacé cherries

1 Stone cherries (unless already done by manufacturers) and return to syrup. Add kirsch.
2 Two-thirds fill sundae glasses with scoops of chocolate ice cream. Coat with cherries and syrup.
3 Top with whipped cream then add a glacé cherry to each. Serve straight away.

Black Forest Gateau

(serves 8 to 12)

Cake Mixture

5oz (150g) self-raising flour (1¼ cups all-purpose plus 3 level tsp double-acting baking powder)

3 level tbsp cornflour (4½ level tbsp cornstarch)

2 level tbsp cocoa powder (3 level tbsp unsweetened cocoa powder)

6oz (175g) butter, slightly softened (¾ cup)

6oz (175g) caster sugar (¾ cup granulated)

1 tsp vanilla essence (1½ tsp vanilla extract)

3 large eggs (kitchen temperature)

3 tbsp cold milk (4½ tbsp)

Filling

1 large can (about 1lb or 450g) black cherries, with stones removed (2 cups)

1½ level tsp cornflour (2 level tsp cornstarch)

4 tbsp kirsch (6 tbsp)

1 pt(575ml) double cream (2½ cups heavy cream)

4 tbsp cold milk (6 tbsp)

4 tbsp caster sugar (6 tbsp granulated)

Decoration

6oz (175g) plain chocolate, grated or coarsely ground in blender or food processor (6 squares)

6 glacé cherries, halved

1 Well-butter two 8in (20cm) sandwich cake tins (pans). Line bases with greased greaseproof paper or non-stick parchment paper. Set oven to 350°F (180°C), Gas 4.

2 Sift flour with cornflour (cornstarch), baking powder if used and cocoa powder. Leave on one side temporarily.

3 Cream butter, sugar and vanilla together until very light in colour and fluffy in texture. Beat in whole eggs, one at a time, adding a tbsp of dry ingredients with each.

4 Using a metal spoon or spatula, fold in rest of dry ingredients alternately with milk. Divide between prepared tins (pans). Bake 30 to 35 minutes or until well risen and golden.

5 Turn out onto wire cooling rack and carefully peel away paper. Leave until completely cold then cut each cake into 2 layers.

6 To make cherry filling, tip cherries and their syrup into saucepan. Place cornflour

126

(cornstarch) into small basin. Add 4 tbsp cherry syrup (6 tbsp) taken from pan. Mix to smooth paste. Return to pan.

7 Cook, stirring all the time, until mixture comes to boil and thickens. Simmer 1 minute. Stir in half the kirsch. Set aside until completely cold.

8 To assemble cake, beat cream, milk and sugar together until thick. Stir in rest of kirsch. Sandwich cake layers together with all the cherry mixture and just over one-third of the cream.

9 Transfer cake very carefully to board or plate. Refrigerate separately both cake and remaining cream, which should be in a covered bowl, for 1 hour.

10 To finish, spread cream thickly over top and sides of cake, leaving enough for decoration. Sprinkle top with chocolate. Press remainder against sides, using a flat-bladed knife.

11 Pipe whirls of cream round top edge then stud each with half a cherry. Refrigerate 2 hours before cutting and serving.

Black Forest Mousse

(serves 4)

1 small can (about 8oz or 225g) black cherries (about 1 cup)
2 tbsp kirsch (3 tbsp)
3½oz (100g) plain chocolate (3½ squares)
2 rounded tsp softened butter (3 rounded tsp)
4 medium-sized eggs, separated (kitchen temperature)
4 heaped tbsp whipped cream, lightly sweetened (6 heaped tbsp)
1 rounded tsp cocoa powder (1½ rounded tsp)

1 Stone cherries (unless already done by manufacturers) and reserve 4 for decoration. Divide remainder, with syrup from can, between 4 wine-type, or sundae, glasses on stems. Add equal amounts of kirsch to each.

2 Break up chocolate. Place, with butter, in basin over hot water. Leave undisturbed until melted, stirring once or twice. Stir in egg yolks. Remove basin from pan and wipe outside dry.

3 Beat egg whites to a stiff snow. Using a large metal spoon or spatula, fold evenly into chocolate mixture.

4 Spoon over cherries in glasses. Chill until firm and set; about 4 to 6 hours. Before serving, top each with cream, sprinkle lightly with cocoa powder then decorate with reserved cherries.

French-style Fruit Savarin

(serves about 10)

Time and effort, yes, but well worthwhile when you see the result!

Yeast Batter
2oz (50g) plain flour ($\frac{1}{2}$ cup all-purpose)
1 level tbsp dried yeast ($1\frac{1}{2}$ level tbsp)
6 tbsp warm milk (9 tbsp)

Basic Savarin Batter
6oz (175g) plain flour ($1\frac{1}{2}$ cups all-purpose)
$\frac{1}{2}$ level tsp salt ($\frac{3}{4}$ level tsp)
1oz (25g) caster sugar ($\frac{1}{8}$ cup granulated)
4 medium-sized eggs, well beaten
$3\frac{1}{2}$oz (100g) butter, softened but not oily (just under $\frac{1}{2}$ cup)

Rum Syrup
$\frac{1}{2}$pt (275ml) water ($1\frac{1}{4}$ cups)
10oz (275g) granulated sugar ($1\frac{1}{4}$ cups)
6 tbsp dark rum (9 tbsp)

Glaze and Filling
3 rounded tbsp apricot jam ($4\frac{1}{2}$ rounded tbsp apricot preserve)
1 tbsp water ($1\frac{1}{2}$ tbsp)
about 1lb (450g) mixed fruit to include halved strawberries, halved and seeded grapes and
pieces of fresh pineapple (16oz)

1 Place all the yeast batter ingredients in large bowl. Leave to stand in a warm place until mixture froths up and looks like a glass of foaming beer; about 30 minutes.

2 Add ingredients listed under Basic Savarin Batter and beat briskly until smooth, allowing 3 to 4 minutes by hand, and half the time if using an electric mixer.

3 Brush a 9in (22.5cm) ring tin with melted white vegetable fat (shortening). Dust very lightly with baking powder as this helps to prevent the dough mixture from sticking to the tin. Transfer batter mixture to prepared tin.

4 Cover with greased greaseproof paper or polythene. Leave to rise in a warm (but NOT hot) place until dough reaches almost to the top of the tin; about 40 to 50 minutes.

5 Bake 20 to 25 minutes in oven preheated to 400°F (200°C), Gas 6. In this time the Savarin should be a warm gold. Remove from oven. Leave in tin 5 minutes then turn out on to a wire cooling rack.

6 To make syrup, pour water into pan. Add sugar. Leave over low heat until sugar dissolves. Bring to boil, and boil 1 minute. Take off heat. Stir in rum.

7 Stand Savarin on large serving dish. Prick all over. Spoon hot syrup over Savarin, reserving about one third. Leave syrup until almost cold.

8 For glaze, melt jam (preserve) slowly with water and brush over Savarin. Mix prepared fruits with reserved syrup and spoon into centre. Serve with pouring cream (coffee cream).

Honey Rum Roulade with Walnuts

(serves 8)

Glamorous and wickedly rich, this is the kind of delight that finds its way onto sweet trolleys of top hotels and restaurants. It isn't the simplest thing in the world to make, so keep it as a reserve when time is not of the essence.

3 large eggs
2 tsp water (3 tsp)
squeeze of lemon juice
3oz (75g) caster sugar ($\frac{3}{8}$ cup granulated sugar)
2 level tbsp honey, melted (3 tbsp)
3$\frac{1}{2}$oz (100g) self-raising flour, sifted twice (just under 1 cup all-purpose plus
2 level tsp double-acting baking powder)
3oz (75g) walnuts, ground (just under $\frac{3}{8}$ cup)

Filling
$\frac{1}{2}$pt (275ml) double cream (1$\frac{1}{4}$ cups heavy cream)
2 level tbsp icing sugar, sifted (3 level tbsp confectioner's sugar)
2 tbsp Bacardi (3 tbsp)
1oz (25g) walnuts, broken into pieces ($\frac{1}{4}$ cup)
4 whole walnut halves for decoration

1 Preheat oven to 400°F (200°C), Gas 6. Brush a Swiss roll tin (pan), measuring 9$\frac{1}{2}$ x 11in (about 24 x 28cm), with melted white cooking fat (shortening). Line base and sides with greaseproof paper. Brush with more fat, then dust with flour.
2 Separate eggs. Beat whites with water and lemon juice until stiff. Gradually add sugar and continue beating until a stiff meringue is formed.
3 Fold in yolks and honey, followed by flour and ground nuts. When smooth and evenly combined, spread into tin.
4 Bake 15 minutes. Remove from oven and turn out on to a sheet of sugared greaseproof paper.
5 Remove lining paper from Roulade, then carefully cut off crusty edges. Cover with a fresh sheet of greaseproof paper and roll up with paper inside. Leave rolled until cold.
6 For filling, beat cream and sugar together until thick and stiff. Stir in Bacardi and broken pieces of walnuts.
7 Uncurl Roulade and remove paper. Spread with walnut filling then re-roll. Stand on serving plate and decorate with walnuts.

Drinks to know and use

Advocaat
Made from eggs and grape brandy, advocaat is a deep yellow drink produced mainly in Holland. Of low alcoholic strength, it is loosely termed a liqueur.

Amaretto di Saronno
Dark gold in colour, this is an Italian liqueur which is flavoured with apricot kernels and tastes mildly of almonds. It is fairly strong and sweet.

Anisette
Sweet liqueur made from aniseed-flavoured spirit, and of medium strength.

Apricot Brandy
A sweet liqueur made from ripe apricots and kernel extracts. A warm amber colour, apricot brandy is moderately strong.

Aquavit
A typically Scandinavian spirit which is very strong. All aquavit is made from either potato or grain spirit flavoured with caraway.

Armagnac
A quality French brandy from Gascony, due south of Bordeaux. Some prefer it to cognac because of its more aromatic flavour.

Bacardi
Almost colourless rum from Puerto Rico. It has a distinctive flavour and is widely used for mixed drinks. It is as strong as whisky.

Bananes, Crème de
A sweet liqueur made from spirit and ripe bananas. It is golden yellow in colour and moderately strong.

Bénédictine
A French herb liqueur, first made four centuries ago to a secret formula. Considered a connoisseur's drink, Bénédictine has an aromatic flavour and is about the same strength as brandy.

Cacao, Crème de
A chocolate-flavoured liqueur of moderate alcoholic strength.

Calvados
Apple brandy made in Calvados, Normandy. It is produced from double distilled apple wine, matured in oak casks. It is as strong as any other brandy.

Campari
A bright red, bitter apéritif originally from Italy, now made in several countries. Based on extract of capsicum and moderately strong.

Cassis, Crème de
A mildly alcoholic blackcurrant liqueur, made in France.

Chartreuse
Brandy-based French herb liqueur, available in green (the original) or yellow varieties; very strong.

Cherry Brandy
Produced internationally, cherry brandy is a mildly alcoholic cherry liqueur, dark red in colour.

Cocoribe
Fairly strong, with a distinct flavour of coconut.

Cognac
Top-class brandy produced in and around the region of Cognac, just north of Bordeaux. It is a mature, strong drink and superior to the straightforward spirit called brandy.

Cointreau
A strong, colourless French liqueur with an orange flavour. It has a high alcohol content and is as strong as whisky.

Curaçao
Liqueur made from spirits and orange peel, as strong as brandy.

Drambuie
A warm and golden-coloured liqueur from Scotland, made from whisky and a secret blend of herbs. It is sweet and strong.

Dubonnet
A wine-based French aperitif of lowish alcoholic strength.

Fraise
A strawberry-flavoured liqueur which is sweet, deep pink in colour and of moderate alcoholic strength.

Framboise
A colourless, dry spirit classed as eau-de-vie. It has a full flavour of raspberries and is produced in France.

Galliano
A strong, Italian liqueur which is bright yellow in colour and made from herbs and spirit. It has a slight liquorice flavour.

Gin
A strong, clear grain spirit flavoured with juniper berries. It is produced worldwide.

Glayva
A whisky-based liqueur with herbs, from Scotland, with a high alcoholic content.

Grand Marnier
This is a mellow, deep honey-coloured liqueur based on cognac and flavoured with orange. Its production began just over a century ago.

Izarra
A brandy-based liqueur flavoured with herbs, from the Pyrenees. It is a strong drink and available both in green or yellow varieties.

Kahlua
A coffee liqueur, originally from Mexico, akin to Tia Maria.

Kirsch
A clear, strong spirit made from cherries. Generally colourless, kirsch is a dry eau-de-vie and produced in Germany, Switzerland and France.

Mandarin Napoléon Liqueur
A sweet, high-strength liqueur flavoured with Andalusian tangerines. It is deep orange in colour and based on eau-de-vie and cognac.

Maraschino
A clear, sweet and strongly-flavoured liqueur based on maraschino cherries and their crushed kernels. It is of medium strength and produced in various European countries.

Marsala
The best known Italian fortified wine, exported for over 200 years. It is amber coloured, sweet, and strongly flavoured.

Mead
Derived from the fermentation of honey, this is one of the oldest alcoholic drinks in the world. The flavour depends on the kind of honey and the addition of various herbs and spices.

Menthe, Crème de
A sweet, peppermint-flavoured liqueur available in two varieties; colourless or emerald green. It is of medium alcoholic strength.

Mirabelle
A French eau-de-vie made from Mirabelle plums. It is colourless, full-flavoured and with a high alcohol content.

Ouzo
Produced in Greece and Cyprus, this is a strong spirit distilled from grape wine and flavoured with aniseed and assorted herbs. Although colourless, it becomes cloudy when water is added.

Parfait Amour
A violet-scented, purple-coloured, sweet and lightly spiced liqueur which is made in slightly different versions throughout Europe.

Pernod

A deep yellow, French apéritif which turns cloudy when mixed with water. It tastes very strongly of aniseed and has a very high alcoholic content.

Pimm's No 1

A gin-based proprietary drink used primarily for cocktails. It is fairly strong.

Raki

A Turkish, aniseed-flavoured spirit similar to ouzo.

Rum

A strong, dry spirit distilled from sugar cane. It can be light gold or deep amber, depending on variety.

Rumvocaat

A variation of advocaat, with Jamaican rum base.

Sambuca Romana

A fairly strong liquorice-flavoured liqueur which is colourless and very sweet.

Sherry

Sherries are fortified wines which start off very pale if dry, deepening in colour as the sherries become sweeter. 'True' sherry should come from Jerez in Spain, but sherries are now being produced all over the world.

Siebrands Cream Liqueur

This is a sweetish, vanilla-flavoured liqueur with the appearance of very creamy white coffee.

Slivovitz

A colourless, plum-flavoured eau-de-vie from Yugoslavia and other Balkan countries. It is a strong spirit and not unlike Mirabelle.

Tequila

A colourless, Mexican spirit produced from the sap of a succulent called agave. It is an excellent mixer drink with a high alcoholic content.

Tia Maria

A medium-strength, light brown liqueur from Jamaica, made from rum and coffee extracts.

Vermouths

These are wine-based apéritifs which are either dry or sweet. They range in colour from very pale to light brown, and are produced mainly in France and Italy.

Vodka

A tasteless, colourless, strong spirit produced from potatoes or grain. Vodka originated in Poland and Russia about 800 years ago.

Index